Beth and Dave speak about a very sensible subject: loss, pain, and suffering. We appreciate this so much because so many people are suffering and nobody wants to talk with them about it. This book will be a good help and an encouragement for many desperate people.

—OLGA BONDARENCO
Way of Hope Events facilitator, social worker in Eastern Europe

This is "rubber meets the road" ministry. This is heart surgery, and Beth and Dave are very qualified to help readers come out victorious on the other side. I strongly recommend *The Way of Hope* to anyone serious about heart healing.

—JOHN BYRNE
mountain region area director, Prison Fellowship

The Way of Hope is a well-written, heartfelt, literary work where Beth and Dave Weikel allow readers to share some of their very private moments. They have divinely designed this anointed blueprint to help individuals find their way to a path paved with hope and healing. You will discover your unique silver lining, even in tragedies.

—PIERRE R. JULIEN
program manager of ministry, Samaritan's Purse

The Way of Hope is a comprehensive manual that walks you through every stage of the process. Drawing from the broad sweep of Scripture, coupled with the depth of their personal experience, the authors leave no stone unturned on the road to recovery and beyond. The proof of the pudding is the authenticity of their lives and the gift of their friendship, a gift I have treasured for four decades.

—BRIAN MORGAN
pastor, Peninsula Bible Church Cupertino

THE WAY OF HOPE

THE **WAY** OF
HOPE

Growing Close to God through Loss

Beth and Dave Weikel

wesleyan
PUBLISHING HOUSE
wphstore.com

Copyright © 2015 by Beth and Dave Weikel
Published by Wesleyan Publishing House
Indianapolis, Indiana 46250
Printed in the United States of America
ISBN: 978-1-63257-050-5
ISBN (e-book): 978-1-63257-051-2

Library of Congress Cataloging-in-Publication Data

Weikel, Beth.
  The way of hope : growing close to God through loss / Beth Weikel, Dave Weikel.
    pages cm
  ISBN 978-1-63257-050-5 (pbk.)
  1. Suffering--Religious aspects--Christianity. 2. Loss (Psychology)--Religious
aspects--Christianity. 3. Spirituality--Christianity. I. Title.
  BV4909.W43 2015
  248.8'6--dc23
                              2015007063

To the Lord, who hears and heals.

"The LORD is near to the brokenhearted and saves those
who are crushed in spirit" (Ps. 34:18).

"The LORD has heard my plea; the LORD accepts my prayer"
(Ps. 6:9 ESV).

"As for me, I shall call upon God, and the LORD will save me.
Evening and morning and at noon, I will complain and
murmur, and He will hear my voice" (Ps. 55:16–17).

"I love the LORD, because He hears my voice and my supplications.
Because He has inclined His ear to me, therefore, I shall
call upon Him as long as I live" (Ps. 116:1–2).

CONTENTS

ACKNOWLEDGEMENTS

We wish to thank those who have supported our outreach and the workshop material in particular. Craig Bubeck, our capable and caring editor at Wesleyan Publishing House, along with his staff of dedicated professionals, have persevered with us to create a unique approach to help those experiencing profound loss and seasons of affliction. We appreciate their sensitivity and commitment to us and our efforts to lead those in need to apply the truths God provides in suffering, who is our source and final authority in these matters.

We also need to mention the many who have attended these workshop events over the years in numerous locales in this country and beyond. Without their vulnerability, we couldn't have honed these materials to fit the broadest possible audience. Our prayers and love extend to them and to numerous others God has allowed to touch our lives and enrich this ministry.

INTRODUCTION
Real Life

A number of years ago, an intense period of loss began that touched our lives in a myriad of ways: a life-threatening illness, the death of our son serving in Iraq, strained family relationships, elder care, the home-going of three parents in less than a year, the miscarriage of a grandchild, a near-fatal car accident involving our other son, a family divorce, a legal crisis, retirement adjustments, financial losses related to the economy's collapse, and various secondary losses arising from these developments. We are learning, because this season is not finished yet, to trust in the faithfulness of our Lord, which may come in unseen ways. He is sovereign. This lesson hasn't come easily, but it was the foundational truth we are determined to claim. We had to; from the beginning, it was the only way we'd make it through.

When deciding to write the first Christmas letter after our losses started to pile up, we knew we would share candidly and transparently. In a few paragraphs, we distilled the contrast between "life then" and "life now." We believed, however, that God's blessings were still with us, but with a darker backdrop. God's intimate presence meant the most, and He was bringing us through.

We closed by saying, "His goodness and mercy are always with us" and by extending an invitation to worship Him in uncertain times. We also quoted the apostle Paul, who said, "Most gladly, therefore, I will rather boast about my weaknesses, so that the power of Christ may dwell in me. [That is why] I am well content with weaknesses, with insults, with distresses, with persecutions, with difficulties . . . for when I am weak, then I am strong" (2 Cor. 12:9–10). In the midst of the pain, those words could sound hollow or even trite. Still, we meant them sincerely. Before we share how we got to that point, and how you can too, along with where our journey of loss led, a few things need to be explained.

IT CAN GET WORSE BEFORE IT GETS BETTER

It's been a few years since we sent that letter and life still challenges us. Unplanned events and their effects on those we care about are not under our control. Living with loss is a delicate balance but also an effective tutor. We don't want these losses to dominate our lives and define us, but they have changed us. We are not the same people as before. In some ways, we are kinder and more sensitive, and in others, less tolerant. We feel more compassion for people, even strangers, experiencing the pain of life when it hurts, and we want to distance ourselves from anything false.

We sense an urgency that doesn't seem to go away. We have only a limited time to reach out with the message God has been developing in us, which is this: He is sufficient for all of life. His ways are holy and right, in spite of circumstances and how others may treat us. We have an Enemy—that is a fact—but we also have divine aid and oceans of comfort for those difficult days we all have to face. God is our treasure, and we still praise Him.

The ministry we've been entrusted with, *by His design*, came out of this struggle to make meaning out of devastating life events. When we itemized the losses which started not that many years ago, it seemed over the top. So now we've learned to focus on the God who takes our hands and walks with us in the midst of pain as well as in its aftermath. He knows the way through any kind of loss, whether large and overwhelming, or smaller but no less significant. He knew we'd need Him for all of life, and He won't desert us.

Let us share some crucial Scripture passages on loss that provide a solid foundation for the journey ahead. We've collected many favorites. In fact, we've discovered nearly every book of the Bible has examples of loss. But we've also seen redemption in every instance, no exception. The Bible is a book of redemption because it's filled with people who need it. It never sugarcoats things. Life is hard, but God is real. The more we live, the more we believe this at the very core.

Our God is no stranger to loss himself. He shares our suffering because He knows what it is to have a broken heart. God the Father invested in humanity to such a degree that He gave all He possessed. Over and over we can witness how God wanted so much for His children, gave so much, while they just wanted their own way. Finally, He sent His own Son, willingly and at great cost, to pay the price for humanity's disobedience and disregard.

But for now, take a look at Moses' desperate statement to this living God: "If Your Presence does not go *with* us, do not bring us up from here . . ." (Ex. 33:15 NKJV, emphasis added). Moses had just come back from Mount Sinai and was carrying the tablets containing the law of God for the children of Israel. Within that law, the Ten Commandments delineated the boundaries of righteous behavior but, more than that, exposed the people's need for their God, who would provide for them. But Moses walked into a mess.

Scripture states, "It came about, as soon as Moses came near the camp, that he saw the calf and the dancing; and Moses' anger burned, and he threw the tablets from his hands and shattered them at the foot of the mountain" (Ex. 32:19).

Moses confronted his brother, Aaron the priest, who was supposed to be in charge in Moses' absence, asking why he had "brought such great sin upon them" (v. 21). Aaron's casual response downplayed their offense and his part in it: "Do not let the anger of my lord burn; you know the people yourself, that they are prone to evil. For they said to me, 'Make a god for us who will go before us; for this Moses, the man who brought us up from the land of Egypt, we do not know what has become of him'" (vv. 22–23).

Apparently, it seemed good to Aaron to tell them to get their gold (plunder from Egypt) and throw it into the fire, "and out came this calf" (v. 24). Life out of control, even on the heels of great blessing.

Moses then gave instructions to the camp and sought the Lord on their behalf to see if he could make atonement for them by offering himself in payment. All along there was a plan: deliver the nation of Israel from bondage in Egypt and take them to the Promised Land. But plans get derailed sometimes.

In response God said He would hold each one accountable and Moses should continue to lead the journey, although an angel would go before them: "For I will not go up in your midst, because you are an obstinate people, and I might destroy you on the way" (Ex. 33:3). Moses again met with God alone and reminded Him how He called Moses by name, "Bring up this people! . . . *Your* people" (vv. 12–13, emphasis added) and also said, "You have also found favor in My sight'" (v. 12). Then God promised, "My presence shall go *with you*, and I will give you rest" (v. 14, emphasis added).

Moses pressed the issue further by stating, "If Your presence does not go with us, do not lead us up from here. For how then can it be known that I have found favor in Your sight, I and Your people? Is it not by Your going with us, so that we . . . may be distinguished from all the other people who are upon the face of the earth?" (vv. 15–16). God was moved and consented.

Moses then made an even greater request: "I pray You, show me Your glory!" (v. 18). This was a critical step. Moses had come this far and had realized his understanding of and closeness to God was key to his fulfilling God's call. God didn't seem put off by this bold request but cautioned He would only let Moses see this in part, or else Moses couldn't survive. "Then the LORD said, 'Behold, there is a place by Me, and you shall stand there on the rock; and it will come about, while My glory is passing by, that I will put you in the cleft of the rock and cover you with My hand until I have passed by. Then I will take My hand away and you shall see My back, but My face shall not be seen'" (vv. 21–23).

What a marvelous scene. How is this similar to when we face times of crisis? I (Beth) can remember finding this verse and mouthing Moses' words, "If Your presence . . ." and "Show me Your glory!" I have come to want that same level of intimacy and care from my Lord. I have boldly asked and have seen Him respond in kind. Even in the low points—especially then. I don't need only what I can see with my eyes, but what my spirit can discern of the living God who is there. I don't just want His angel, though that is wonderful. I want Him.

If God knows my name and has called me to follow Him in all that life can be, I want much more. And I haven't been disappointed. As I face those discouraging times when all I can do is lean harder and harder on Him though fear and dread lurk ever so close, I know His hand puts me on the rock and places me in that safe and sacred space with Him. There He shows me what only He can be. I hear Him proclaiming His name to me, and I see His goodness, though nothing outside this experience has changed. I have found Him to be a compassionate and gracious Lord to me, and one day I *will* see His face.

We invite you to join us on the road that leads to hope, even in the midst of loss. In the coming chapters, we'll take a hard look at the realities of loss, explore what Scripture says about it, and discover how to not only survive, but find renewed meaning and purpose for our lives. While we will candidly share from our experiences, it's essential that you delve into yours as well.

Personal reflection questions in each chapter will help you process and grow. Based in scriptural truth, these questions, intended to be answered in a journal, can be a meaningful part of your journey at this time. Since we seek to dig deep, these reflective times begin as we *excavate* and search the Word of God, *extend* or stretch ourselves by applying the truth to our lives, and *emerge* as we look toward trans-formation (based on Col. 2:6–10). We encourage you to take time with these questions and not rush past them.

Additionally, the first few chapters include journal activities separate from the personal reflections. These will help you prepare to receive the truths shared in the book. Again, please take time to let God speak to you through them. These activities can help carry the load just a little further as we journey together to find that safe place in the rock where we can see God.

WHAT LOSS INTRODUCES

We celebrated forty years of marriage in the summer of 2015 by inviting friends from far and wide to an evening in our garden, complete with a multimedia slide show we put together depicting the seasons of a marriage. We wanted to keep it manageable in length, so we were selective. We also reflected on the intimacy of life in marriage and family life by including memorable quotes by authors, ranging from fairly obscure modern ones to the classics.

Stages of our life together flashed by: the wedding ceremony, packing to leave our parents' houses to make a new home for ourselves while still college students, the birth of our two boys and their growing years, a few holidays, camping trips, graduations, and finally the transition to the empty nest with an active retirement filled with new pursuits. We accompanied this with the soundtrack of a lesser-known Broadway play called *I Do, I Do* and its funny, poignant, very realistic lyrics about domestic life; fascinating and familiar at the same time.

So many of us often live predictable lives. In the course of long-term married experience, each couple will have their share of exhilaration, their portion of pathos, and ample doses of the mundane. Life is about sameness *and* change and how we deal with both.

Most of us have firsthand knowledge of new love, married love, childbirth, parenthood, career building, home ownership, and retirement planning, as well as extended family outings and celebrations along the way. Yet there is no escaping the fact that these same milestones have equally weighty counterpoints: divorce, remarriage, blended families with awkward adjustments, rebellious children, serious or chronic illness, caregiving for elderly parents, death (whether expected or sudden), job loss and career change, financial crises, home foreclosure or eviction, deployments and disability (for military populations), and for some, even the incarceration of a family member. Nothing is out of the realm of possibility.

These life challenges, even the pleasant ones, can involve loss. Our grown children marry and move away, we downsize, we retire, and so on. Our minds and accompanying emotions must do some work to catch up. We can't just stay where we are and pretend nothing has happened. If we are honest, we could identify some fear or sadness, even anger. Often, though, we expect that we can just roll along and time will take care of things.

But in many cases, like ours, dramatic events happen, one after another, until we think we may never feel whole again. We long for what we had. We cry out for relief, refreshment, and renewal and may not even know the "next steps." Life feels overwhelming, and there's no letup. Our hearts have been broken by life in all its dimensions. We battle just to get up and face another day. What is the point? Too much has been taken away, and we don't seem to have many choices left.

Been there? Still there? There is a life beyond loss. Life is not over and there are answers, but finding them will require specific strategies and a willingness to rebuild on what's left. There are tools to unpack and resources available. We trust that's encouraging news. To know that you still matter and someone cares who cares can help is vital.

SURRENDER, A PARADOX

Although perhaps right now such words ring flat and even sound harsh, for you feel trapped in the minor key of life. But you don't have to stay stuck. All you have to do is begin right where you are. This part is where you accept God's act of grace that doesn't demand anything but a desire to hear some truths and see where the help is going to come from.

I (Beth) call it *surrender*. At one point, I confessed to an acquaintance, "I only have the strength to surrender." That's the starting place, the safe refuge, the end of pretending, and the beginning of life now. Life will be full and rich again. It's a promise from the heart of God.

Life can cause us to lose our way, break us, and beat us down so we can't look up anymore. Many of us have seen this happen to someone or heard about someone who has experienced this. In the crushing times, the unplanned-for times, we need a proven foundation that won't rock when all around us does. It's natural in trying times to look for someone to blame. Many shake their fists at an unknown, unseen deity, or at someone even closer in their lives. We want to hold someone responsible for our pain. Someone needs to pay. Our real enemy rarely receives this blame. However, living with brokenness doesn't require that we inflict a wound on a convenient bystander. That won't bring healing anyway. It certainly didn't help the Israelites, which is clear from their wilderness days. They determined to hold someone responsible—usually Moses.

Moses learned many lessons about dealing with blame while wandering in the desert with the nation of Israel. Whenever a shortage occurred, fingers pointed and tongues wagged in his direction. The people were headed to the Promised Land and knew it, but the journey was harder and longer than they imagined. In Exodus 17, they ran out of water (again) and feared that they were at the end, asking, "Why, now, have you brought us up from Egypt, to kill us and our children and our livestock with thirst?" (v. 3).

Moses did the wise thing and cried out to God for an answer to their problem: "What shall I do to this people? A little more and they will stone me" (v. 4). God told Moses to take his staff (the same one used to part the Red Sea), gather some elders, and pass before the people. God would be standing before him at the rock of Horeb, which he was to strike with the staff so water would gush out for the people to drink. After this was accomplished for all to see, Moses named the place Massah (test) and Meribah (quarrel), "because they tested the LORD, saying, 'Is the LORD among us, or not?' " (v. 7).

Adversity can create conflicts with God and others. Many times we don't turn to the Lord, who knows the solution; we just try to run our own show. We mistrust His leadership when times are tough and dreams are dashed. Then the Enemy comes and takes advantage. However, when we look to God instead of laying blame, miraculous things can happen.

Moses and Joshua witnessed this in the closing verses of Exodus 17. Amalek was on the march against Israel. Moses told Joshua to choose some men for battle and he would station himself within view on top of a nearby hill with his staff, "the staff of God" (v. 9), in his hand. The battle ensued and raged on and on. If Moses let down the staff, the enemy prevailed, so Aaron and Hur aided Moses, whose hands grew weary holding up the staff as the day wore on. They worked as a team and "Joshua overwhelmed Amalek" (v. 13).

Immediately following this victory for Israel, God told Moses to "write this in a book as a memorial and recite it" (v. 14). He wanted His people to remember what took place and what the Lord "has sworn" (v. 16). So Moses built an altar on that site and named it "The Lord is My Banner" (v. 15).

Some of the choices Moses made in this situation need to be recognized for our benefit as well. Faith in overwhelming circumstances is the right response. It's not the natural one, but the best one. Also, rather than panicking and looking for a scapegoat, we should instead build a team and do battle together. The body of Christ is uniquely designed for this purpose. Diversity and unity are its strengths. And when the worst is behind us, it's not a bad idea to record the victory and give glory to God, who was in our midst. He is our banner and our only hope in the onslaught. How can we connect with the living God's promises in authentic ways and experience renewal and growth to ensure our trials aren't for nothing? God's purposes, as we've seen so far, are for salvation and wholeness. That is the direction He leads us in, though the battle may be raging.

Learning to do battle through grief by using a recovery plan is a practical strategy for real life today. We don't have to wait until we feel like having faith. Faith will be provided when we invite our faithful God into the dreaded mess, the unexplainable, the awful alarm, the solitary place of longing. God will offer acceptance, assurance, and almighty power. He is able to bring life from loss.

Since the one constant in this life is change, we must learn to find meaning in difficult times, when life unravels. We'll look at practical help in dealing with loss on a number of levels, including mental, emotional, and spiritual. In the next few chapters, you'll be led through a series of journaling activities that help you explore your own story and gain understanding amidst the pain and confusion of significant loss. Before we set out together, it's important to understand the goal of these activities and to reflect on a few key questions in advance.

PURPOSEFUL BROKENNESS

Because life challenges us with episodes of loss, we must become skilled and committed to handling all of life from the perspective of what we call purposeful brokenness. God's grace operates in our brokenness with the long view in mind, while actively, intimately embracing His sons and daughters in a lasting embrace — day by day.

Three questions need to be addressed before we proceed. One reveals awareness of our loss, another exposes the burden(s) it brings, and the last considers a step of action for coping in the midst:

1. Why am I studying this topic? What made me decide to pick up this book and look at the issue of loss?
2. What is my biggest challenge (or series of challenges)?
3. How am I praying about that?

By answering these three questions, you will find a starting place from which to move forward. Your willingness to respond to them shows a sense of determination, however slight, that you are ready to go to work. We know how hard it is to get up in the morning and say, "I want to deal with my brokenness." We are the same way. We know how difficult it is to be proactive about our brokenheartedness. But by taking this on, you are committing to work on recovery and focus on life. Consider this process an opportunity to walk through your pain with us and Jesus Christ. He will be the faithful and able one. We find Him in the Word of God and will use it to support our points and examples. This book is interactive, not just a quick read, because it takes work to live with loss and recover our lives.

Since we can't escape loss in our lives, what is God's plan for it? That's what we'll explore together. But first, please take a moment to pray for God's Spirit to come alongside and be your teacher. Give Him your feelings and doubts, and ask Him to impart understanding to you and reward your willingness to investigate His truth as it applies to your loss. Lay the mess at His feet and expect Him to take up your burden. Anticipate His work, and say yes to the process. Most of all, let Him wrap you safely in His love and strength. He's been waiting to meet you here.

God is personally acquainted with loss. On a large scale, He repeatedly experienced heartbreak over the nation of Israel as they rebelled and embraced idolatry, disregarding the many times He rescued them and took constant care of them. On a more personal level, God sacrificed His only Son, Jesus, when Jesus died a criminal's death on a cross of shame. Though some accept this dramatic sacrifice and join the family of God, many others reject this offering and choose to live apart from Him.

Throughout the Scriptures, God referred to Israel as a stiff-necked people, meaning they stubbornly followed their own desires and acted in disobedience. When we read this description, we feel God's pain. This is the same nation He redeemed from slavery and exile, led through the wilderness for decades with a cloud by day and a pillar of fire by night, then finally settled in a land He chose to give them to prosper in. He worked miracles in their sight and brought them out of an oppressive place.

In response the children of Israel complained, doubted His goodness, and worshiped other gods instead of following Him, the one true God. After a series of warnings from the prophets about their practices, the children of Israel again were displaced for a season until God brought them back. Throughout these times, He never abandoned them and kept all His promises.

This same God is willing to go the distance with us and has provided all we need to accomplish this. His compassion, mercy, and power are the same today. Will we let Him lead us, or will we stubbornly try to go our own way? Do we want His help?

2

GUIDEPOSTS FOR THE JOURNEY

With the questions from the previous chapter answered, we're ready to move forward. Here are some truths to keep in mind as we proceed: First, the thing we want God to do—and what we have seen Him do in the past—is to bring life from loss. Loss is a fact of life. It is something we can't escape in our fallen world. Yet God is capable of bringing life from each loss, though that does not mean our emotions necessarily follow right away. That eventually happens through His work in our hearts and lives.

Next, we are reassured when we remember the truth that He is bringing a message from our mess. Some of us are living with a mess. Some of us have been living with a mess for some time, and God is preparing that message. Whether you realize it or not, you are living that message. People may even sometimes tell you, "Hey, I have noticed [insert something positive or a change] about you." Consider that an encouragement. What they mean, we trust, is that they see God in you. What better thing than to have God's life displayed in us?

The Bible is full of brokenness. We can't turn to a book in the Bible anymore and not see brokenness. But we can also see redemption. In the Scriptures, we can see God working in a situation and in someone's life to help with loss. It's as if He's saying, "Yes, I know this is tough, but we are not done, and there are so many promises." *Promises.* That is not an idle, empty word to us anymore. There are so many promises and evidence of their fulfillment.

The deeper time of journaling that follows is meant to help you connect to the Lord and let Him bring to the surface what He wants to assist you with. You can come back to this journaling at any time, and we hope that you do. You have this resource now, and you are going to get a sense of how to start putting things together using the Scriptures.

Another concept, actually a little catch phrase we like, is "grief relief." We will not always feel the burden in the exact way we do now. God promises to bring relief if we allow Him to. For our part, when we deal with something as difficult as processing loss, we must believe we *are* going to get some sense of relief. We need to trust God with that, though understanding this might be just the beginning of our healing.

One way to begin learning to trust God is by exploring the implications of loss in other lives. You are *not* alone. God is not picking on you. So then what is God's plan? (Because He has a plan.) Is He here? That's what we should look at and we'll say with conviction even now, "Yes, He is here."

ACTIVITY 1

To begin, simply list as many words as you can associate with the word *loss*. Brainstorm what comes to mind when you think of that word and write it all down. Try to generate as many words as you can. Whatever comes to mind is fine.

What are some of the responses you came up with? Some examples are: *anger*, *emptiness*, *void*, *confusion*, *encumbered*, *abandonment*, *unnecessary*, *heaviness*, *failure*, *betrayal*, and *fear*. Perhaps even *ouch!* may have occurred to you. We need to be honest, don't we? This is how it feels.

I (Beth) was studying Isaiah 38, the section where Hezekiah became ill, turned his face to the wall, and prayed to God. He said, in effect, "Remember how I have walked before You in truth, with a whole heart? I don't want to die." Because of this prayer, God performed a miracle. God heard his prayer and granted him fifteen more years. I didn't know this before, but Hezekiah was only thirty-nine years old when this happened. He was not an old man. In Isaiah 38, he was in touch with the Lord, and he wrote a song to God after his life was extended: "I felt deprived, ripped off. I felt all these things because my life would be taken prematurely. . . . Be my security, O Lord, I am oppressed. . . . Let me live" (Isa. 38:10–20, paraphrase). It is a great thing to see in Scripture where God allows such honest expression.

Now, a hard question to answer: Are there any words on your brainstorming list that seem positive? Maybe you have these words or phrases: *starting over*, *forgiveness*, *growth*, or *dependence on God*.

What we want to introduce here is that there is purpose. Regardless of outcomes, there is going to be an aim, an intentional resolution of eternal significance. This doesn't minimize the pain or negate the difficulties, however. It simply says, by faith, we can still trust God's plan. Somehow, these times have value and meaning. Some of us are in an intense period of suffering. Some of us are past our suffering, but we do not know what to do with that time in our lives and its lingering impact. During this God says gently and compassionately, "Keep trusting. My plans have purpose."

After our son, Ian, was killed in Iraq, we had several memorial services, not only in Texas, but also in Colorado Springs and then at Arlington Cemetery, where we had the funeral. This period took at least two weeks, and, fortunately, I (Beth) had that numbing sensation through some of this, so I didn't feel the whole weight of it. Within a week after we got home, I was calling my daughter-in-law, now a widow. I was instinctively asking her questions: "How are you holding up? Is God's presence evident yet for you?"

She was not ready for those questions. All I wanted to tell her was that was what my expectation was for God and me. I wanted to see it and was searching for it. When He showed up with grace in any form, I did not want to miss it. I shared with her, "This is what I saw of Him today: I got out of bed, I took a walk, and I got some exercise." You want to be able to identify for yourself something positive that is happening. That is what grace means.

GRACE IN TIMES OF LOSS

Lamentations 3:22–23 is a passage to commit to memory. The book of Lamentations is Jeremiah's journal, and he was expressing his thoughts about his ministry to the children of Israel while they continued to rebel, worship idols, and reject God. When they were taken captive, Jeremiah journaled: "The LORD's lovingkindnesses indeed *never* cease, for His compassions *never* fail. They are new *every* morning; great is your faithfulness" (emphasis added).

The term *lovingkindness* can mean "loyal love." Don't you love that? Some Bible versions translate *lovingkindness* as "mercies that never cease." They never run out. God's compassion and lovingkindness are new every single morning. That is a promise. Whether we feel it or not, and we will have those days where there is no way we are going to feel it, this promise is something we can hold on to.

People have told us concerning the loss surrounding our son, "There is a hole in your heart, and it will always be there. It is always going to be raw, like a sore that never heals." We don't believe this. This is not how we've seen our God work. Why would this loss be an exception? Though we will fully feel our grief and experience the pain of separation, that's part of the process. It's part of how God heals the wound.

Even so, James 1 initially feels somewhat problematic when we look at suffering. It says, "Count it all joy" (James 1:2 ESV). *Joy* is an odd word. What joy? Why joy? What we've learned in Bible study is that when reading Scripture, if something doesn't seem to fit, we may need to keep reading. If we do, we will often come upon the purpose, the goal—and this is the joy part: God will make us complete.

What I (Beth) saw in James 1 is that trials test our faith, and if I continue to walk with Jesus, He will give me the endurance I need. That is the key. Am I going to keep my hand in His, or am I going to shake it off? If we keep reading through the book of James, we see that we will get that perfection, which means all God is doing is part of making us complete. During our struggles, we allow ourselves to be clay and Him to be the sculptor.

However, James 1 presents a tough place for us to go. It is not meant to be applied like a bandage. It's not meant to fix things instantly or just cover them up. That wouldn't bring healing to deep wounds. But the Scripture and its truth might be something to meditate on. When we do, we might pray, "God, I am going to trust You for this. I am not sure how this is going to happen, but I like that You want to make me complete, lacking in nothing." No one can get through this life without experiencing loss. God must have a way to help us through it.

THE ILLUSIONS OF LOSS

We have learned that, depending on their belief systems, many people refuse to acknowledge these times of loss and just keep going. They think, "It was bad, but it is not a big deal." However, it still haunts them. Instead, God wants us to pay attention, talk to Him about it, and let Him talk to us. We need to assign significant meaning to those times, whether our loss occurs through sickness, divorce, death, or some other tragedy. All these losses challenge us in our relationships with other people and with our Lord.

However, through the numbness, disbelief, and crushing feelings, we must realize the way we view reality and confront the many illusions people often live with.

Some of those illusions arise from unnecessary emotions. For example, maybe we feel guilty, which has led us to believe, incorrectly, that things were our fault. Although guilt may be part of the grieving process, we can move beyond that and see things accurately again, through God's eyes. There could also be fear that we don't know how to get past.

We need to express real emotions and actually face the pain, not avoid it. We needed to lean into that pain because that was when we find God's strength. What we all need to do is to walk with Jesus and let His love and words continue to be applied to the situations we are really struggling with. His love, comfort, and guidance are invaluable. We must face what is real and acknowledge what is false.

HOW TO FACE WHAT IS REAL

There are two concepts to remember about facing reality. First, you still have choices in loss. You have choices every day. They may be big or small, but they are your choices.

Second is the concept of knowing. Ask yourself, what do I still know? Even if it doesn't *feel* true at the moment, what can I stand on regardless of my emotions and all the temptations I have to just run away? What do I still know that doesn't change? When I read the Scriptures, there are certain places where this concept truly jumps out, so look for *choices* and *knowing* in Scripture.

Especially important to remember, however, is that you are not alone. You may have feelings and physical sensations surrounding your event—that's normal—and these may feel like they will continue from now until eternity, but God has a set time for these trials, even if it doesn't seem like it at the moment. Because of the feelings that come with trials, a person's temptation is to isolate. You might think, "I can't share this with anyone. I can't even face it myself. I am probably the only one." The fact that you are reading this book or participating in a workshop is proof that you are not the only one. Others are joining you on the journey.

Hagar and Ishmael found out they were not alone in the wilderness. When elderly Abraham and Sarah were anticipating God's promised miracle baby, they could not wait for God. Eventually, Sarah developed her own plan: Hagar. "We have a handmaiden. I am very old, and she is not; so why don't you have a baby with her," Sarah said in effect to her husband (Gen. 21:9–17, 21).

However, as often happens with our plans, this created even more complications. It was not what God wanted for them. God wanted them to be patient and wait for His timing. Going ahead with their plan created a domestic situation no one could live with. Consequently, Abraham found himself wondering what he should do. Sarah decided Abraham needed to send Hagar out with her son into the wilderness. "We can't have this tension," Sarah may have remarked. By this time Isaac was born and Sarah felt threatened because Ishmael was the firstborn. God said to Abraham, "'Do not be distressed because of the lad and your maid; whatever Sarah tells you, listen to her, for through Isaac your descendants shall be named. And of the son of the maid I will make a nation also, because he is your descendant.' So Abraham rose early in the morning and took bread and a skin of water and gave them to Hagar, putting them on her shoulder, and gave her the boy, and sent her away" (vv. 12–14).

The wilderness in that part of the world is bare. There is nothing there. It will not sustain life. After a time, Hagar's rations were gone. The story continues this way: "And she departed and wandered about in the wilderness of Beersheba. When the water in the skin was used up, she left the boy under one of the bushes. Then she went and sat down opposite him, about a bowshot away, for she said, 'Do not let me see the boy die.' And she sat opposite him, and lifted up her voice and wept" (vv. 14–16).

In this part of the world, people don't just whimper and whine; they wail! This is real grief, from the depth of one's being. Scripture says, "God heard the lad crying." That is significant. It goes on: "And the angel of God called to Hagar from heaven and said to her, 'What is the matter with you, Hagar? Do not fear, for God has heard the voice of the lad where he is'" (v. 17).

There is more to this account, but essentially, Hagar and Ishmael received blessing. God did not forget about them and they prospered. In the middle of absolute nowhere, "God heard the lad crying" (v. 17). God listened to Hagar's voice. God said, "I still have a plan." Don't be tempted to feel all alone, because this is the same God we know today.

PERSONAL REFLECTION

Open your journal and take some time to dig deep with God through the following exercises.

Excavate: deepening our roots. Read Romans 8:35–39; 2 Samuel 12:15–23; and 18:31–33.

Extend: branching out. Is it possible for trials to separate us from God's love? Often tears come, but that's a part of healing. Tears let the soul empty its well of sadness. Can you allow yourself to cry? When emotions are triggered, is there some internal inhibition that prevents their release? What is that inhibition?

Emerge: looking ahead. What is God saying to you in this chapter? What will you do in response? As you look for this, how did you see this in action in your heart or life? (Provide an example and the date.)

ACTIVITY 2

Make a list of the losses you are walking with today. As you make a list, ask God to reveal those losses, especially if you have been trying to ignore some of them. Next to each one, identify its significance and the emotions associated with it. Don't rush through this. Don't hold anything back from God; He'll help you do this.

In our discussion so far, we have seen how God is clearly very involved in all aspects of our lives, including our times of loss. God himself is acquainted with the experience and feelings of loss. Others, in every part of the globe and in all times, are walking this path, yet some aren't allowing God to help. This may be because they are held captive by illusions associated with difficult times. These may include assumptions about others' responses, as well as how God should behave, and more.

The Scriptures are full of examples of God leading individuals of any station in life through loss and into life. When we invite Him to look at what's been happening to us, we can safely move ahead and start healing. Healing is available because there is hope.

3

THE POINT OF SUFFERING

When we talk about suffering, sooner or later Job comes up. Most of us know what happened to Job. He got up one day like any other and had a life-changing experience. Everything came crashing down all at once.

What others still respond to in this ancient account is how Job's suffering and loss transformed him. For most of the book of Job, we witness how one person goes through extreme loss day after day, and comes out on the other side. We're taken behind the scenes to the cause of his suffering, which was the central question that plagued those directly involved in it, and a source of great misunderstanding on the part of many who knew Job.

The Bible calls Job a righteous man. In Job 1, we read of God's conversation with Satan, in which God referred to Job as "blameless and upright. . . . My servant" (Job 1:1, 8 NIV). God allowed all that happened in order to test Job's faith. The first thing Job did when he received the news of losing all ten of his children and his large amount of livestock, leaving behind just him and his wife, was in response to this test: "Then Job arose and tore his robe and shaved his head [expressions of grief], and he fell to the ground and worshiped" (v. 20).

Worshiped? That seems odd, doesn't it? Under these circumstances, Job said, "Naked I came from my mother's womb, and naked I shall return there. The LORD gave and the LORD has taken away. Blessed be the name of the LORD" (v. 21).

From Job's perspective, it all came from God's hand. Many of us sing Matt Redman's song "Blessed Be Your Name" in church with similar words: "You give and take away, you give and take away. My heart will choose to say, 'Lord, blessed be Your name.'" This idea originates from the life of Job. "Through all this Job did not sin nor did he blame God" (v. 22). The fact that Job did not blame God for all his pain and suffering is incredible.

Now let's look at Job 2. God and Satan had another discussion in which Satan said in effect, "Yeah, but if You touch his body, I am sure he will feel differently." So, Job was given a horrible disease with lots of pain and discomfort, and no one knew any way to heal him. His suffering became very personal. "Then Satan went out from the presence of the LORD and smote Job with sore boils from the sole of his foot to the crown of his head" (v. 7).

Job took a "potsherd" (v. 8), which is a piece of pottery, and scraped his oozing sores. While he was sitting among the ashes like an outcast at the city dump, his wife came to him and said, "Do you still hold fast your integrity? Curse God and die!" (v. 9).

She was essentially saying, "End it; just end it, Job. I do not see any way out." There are a couple different ways to interpret her words: (1) She felt compassion for Job and hated to see him suffer, or (2) she herself had experienced all the same losses and could see no way out. Maybe her bitterness was speaking as well.

Job's response was quick and wise: "You speak as one of the foolish women speaks. Shall we indeed accept good from God and not accept adversity?' In all this Job did not sin with his lips" (v. 10).

What a concept! Should we only accept good? Is that who we serve—a God who gives us only good things? Shouldn't we also accept adversity from His hand? The only possible way we can do this is to know more about this God.

Now let's look at Job 3. Here we can see such honesty. God did not just include happy stories or people acting like puppets. Notice what happened to Job when prolonged suffering took its toll: "Afterward Job opened his mouth and cursed the day of his birth. . . . 'Let the day perish on which I was to be born. . . . May that day be darkness; let not God above care for it, nor light shine on it. . . . Why did I not die at birth, come forth from the womb and expire? . . . For what I fear comes upon me, and what I dread befalls me. I am not at ease, nor am I quiet, and I am not at rest, but turmoil comes'" (vv. 1, 3–4, 11, 25–26).

Have you been there? That is what despair looks like when people hit the bottom. They ask, "Why was I even born? Why was God so mean to give me life if this is what life is?" In chapter 3, Job fully expressed his despair. His raw suffering is hard to look at, but it was necessary for him to honestly cry out his helpless longings. It's even more necessary for us to consider life in all dimensions, positive and negative.

When trials and tragedy descend on us, churning comes: "What if . . . ? If only . . ." All kinds of questions plagued Job. They plague us. It's important to look at Job and not see just the man at the end of the book, where everything was handed back to him, twice and then some. We don't have that guarantee with some of the losses we are walking with. No, we need to look intently at his brokenness—a man with a broken heart, a broken body, and a broken life.

We should also read the rest of the book and notice how his friends came to help but didn't know how to. Have you had that experience?

Here is a myth you might have heard before: "Time heals all wounds." Are you good with that? Time helps sometimes when you get some distance from an event but it doesn't necessarily heal all wounds. Wounds that have been yielded to a God who cares and who has the power to do something about them, who knows us and loves us, those are the wounds that heal.

So you tell Him the problems and invite Him in: "Please come into this disappointment, this fear, this anxiety, this awful thing." Some of us just give up and put those things away without letting God complete the process to wholeness. As we come to know God better, our faith in Him sustains and moves us forward. As you read the Word and let the Word be applied, you move forward. Your progress comes in little steps, however, not all at once. This is the "refining" the Bible talks about.

As a result, we can feel the sorrow. We don't deny our feelings, yet we still believe. We believe the truth that is there, which clarifies our vision. Sometimes when I (Beth) am having one of those days, I realize it's time to open my Bible to look for something I know is true. I'll look expectantly until I find something, maybe a psalm. As I read the psalm, I'll see again who God is, who I am, and that we are not done yet. Using these resources restores my perspective.

PERSONAL REFLECTION

Excavate: deepening our roots. Read Job 40:1–6.

Extend: branching out. Have you found yourself arguing with God? How have you found perspective again? Have you been silent before God (and His Word) so He can speak to you?

Emerge: looking ahead. What is God saying to you about this? What will you do? As you look for this, how did you see this action in your heart or life? (Provide an example and the date.)

If you are having a hard time, 1 Peter is a great book to read. From beginning to end, 1 Peter is about suffering. It is also about hope in suffering. There are going to be those times of fiery ordeals, and we are to entrust our soul to our faithful Creator, the One who knows it is happening and has a way through.

We have a choice, right? We can listen to that voice that seeks to drag us down, or we can bring that thought captive to Christ and say, "Is that from You? Is that the truth? Is that what I'm really supposed to hang on to?" And many times that thought will evaporate.

We are not alone. We are suffering along with all the believers in the faith. People we have never met are in the same place we are.

Now more than ever, we feel like we're in this race, and we're not done yet. God is entrusting us with more and more. We have hard-won hope because we are willing to say, "OK, I will trust You in this." We have a choice in each instance. Each day we can accept His help. We can ask for it. Suffering is meant to connect us to God. We should ask for His strength so we can become the people He designed us to be.

One of the things you'll notice when you get to this place of acceptance is that you can say, "I need help. I need Your strength. I have none left." One of the benefits of this will be that He will open your eyes, and you'll look around to see other people out there. It's not just all about you and how much you hurt. You'll find yourself in situations where you can offer a genuine word of hope to others who are hurting or simply live your life in front of them. This is a part of the calling. We learn to trust our Lord and can show others from experience that it works.

PERSONAL REFLECTION

Excavate: deepening our roots. Read 2 Corinthians 1:3–5.

Extend: branching out. How did Paul refer to God in 2 Corinthians 1:3–5? What are we promised? What is the goal? What two kinds of abundance can we expect?

Emerge: looking ahead. What is God saying to you about this Scripture? What will you do? As you reflect on this passage, how have you seen these principles at work in your life? As you look for this, how did you see this action in your heart or life? (Provide an example and the date.)

Second Corinthians 4:7–18 uses the phrase "don't lose heart." That wording isn't just a command to obey; it comes with a promise of enabling. We are earthly vessels, mere fragile pots. It is bad, but it's not hopeless. Therefore, don't be surprised that you are carrying around the death of Jesus, because He wants to give you His life, that same resurrection life. What is He calling you to? There is a purpose in there somewhere. It's embedded. What desires do you have? Even now there are some desires, but what excuses are you making to postpone those things?

ACTIVITY 3

Identify your desires and dare to dream again. For some of us, this may seem a little premature. We can't imagine that we even get to dare to dream again. But let's put ourselves in a place where we can think, "If I didn't have this problem, I could just focus on that dream. Regardless of finances, or the time I have available, or the necessary strength of will which I don't seem to have, or the lack of any developed talent, or other perceived barriers, what would I want to do about this dream?" Pray and invite God into this venture, asking Him to clarify the dream and the priorities you have at present. It will take faith in Him and belief in yourself.

Sometimes we see ourselves as an extension of someone else—our family, for instance. You might say, "I can have that dream when my kids are grown" or "I can have that dream when I finish caring for my elderly parent." We are not an extension of someone else in that sense. We still get to have our own dream from God, who will find a way to make that dream happen—if we pay attention to it.

With all that in mind, what do you know about God and about His Word that propels you forward? How has He worked in the past in your own life? We all have those experiences where we can look back and see what He did for us.

In John 21, Jesus and Peter were on the seashore. Jesus had already been to the cross and was now resurrected. He was trying to put things in place before He ascended into heaven to be with the Father in order that the work would continue. We find that Jesus and Peter were talking about the kind of death Peter could be facing. Jesus reminded Peter that one day someone would be leading him where he didn't want to go, but he was to follow

Jesus (John 21:18–19). Jesus continued to remind Peter to give Him control.

We are no different from Peter. We are a part of the whole story that God is writing. Our only requirement is to follow. We don't always know what this means, but we have to be willing. This is the discussion Peter and Jesus had. The point of this passage is that Peter was redeemed. Peter probably thought he could not be redeemed. He probably thought there was no future for him in this kingdom work.

Later, though, in the book of Acts, we see Peter possessing incredible strength and an amazing gift. He stood for Christ. He told anyone present, in very definite terms, who Jesus was, what they needed to do about it, and how Jesus could make a difference in their lives.

As we can see from Peter's experiences, none of these trials we face are meant to knock us out of the game. In Acts 3, Peter and John were walking toward the temple and came across a beggar. The beggar obviously wanted money. Peter said, "I do not possess silver and gold, but what I do have I give to you: In the name of Jesus Christ the Nazarene—walk!" (v. 6).

What do we do with that? Help the sidelined. We can give people Jesus, and they can rise and walk. It's not about material things. As you experience this dare-to-dream process, think outside the box. How can Jesus live through you? It's what He came to do.

4
INCLUDING OTHERS

Now that we've opened up the possibility of dreaming new dreams, it may be a good time to look around and see what else, or who else, is on the landscape. I (Beth) am so grateful that Dave and I had invested in friends before this intense season of loss arrived. People, by and large, have been part of the comfort and growth we've experienced during this time. God is using our relationships in special ways.

The question here is who else cares? We know God cares, but who else? Has your loss impacted others in your life? Has God used someone to encourage you in your circumstances? Are you open to seeing God's hand in this way, or do you push people away?

Because of what has happened to us, our relationships have been affected to the point that we can be an inspiration to some or a discomfort to others. People either don't know what to do with you or instead imply, "When I face that, I sure want to be like you." One can either be the "fragrance of Christ" that 2 Corinthians 2:15–16 talks about or that of the "aroma from death to death." Depending on where people are themselves spiritually, they will perceive it as life-giving or avoid it all together. The very hope we have, if in fact we are walking in it, can be offensive.

ACTIVITY 4

Try to remember the ways others have shown love to you in the wake of your loss or difficulty. Who, specifically, is God using in this way? What words and actions have been expressed? How have they helped? Include this in your journal and thank God for this.

Other times people mean well, but their efforts have not always been a good thing. Their words or actions have fallen short. Or it might be that some circumstance God has allowed into your life elicits an outright negative response from others. Some may even judge you because of a loss you've experienced, thinking or even saying, "You must not have much of a relationship with the Lord if that is going on in your life."

What expectations do we have for other people in these situations? Do you expect other people to come to you all the time and bring flowers, call you, or send nice notes without you asking? Take some time to outline this and pray about it. Pay attention to what God is teaching you.

PERSONAL REFLECTION

Excavate: deepening our roots. Read Mark 14:1–9; 1 Corinthians 4:9–13; Philippians 1:12–20; 2:19–22, 25–27; and Acts 11:19–26.

Extend: branching out. In the above Scripture references, notice where people are encouraged and where they are judged. It doesn't always matter if we're doing the right thing or not. We can be misunderstood. How do some of these verses say that God has it covered and that good will result?

Emerge: looking ahead. What is God saying to you about this? What will you do? As you look for this, how did you see this action in your heart or life? (Provide an example and the date.)

Let me (Dave) mention something we didn't plan on that was helpful for us. I have a slightly unusual hobby. I have this apparatus, parked in the garage, that has a parachute and an engine. I love to fly it. A friend talked me into it, which wasn't difficult and it's not all that expensive, as hobbies go.

Not long after our lives took a nosedive, this same friend called and asked, "Should we go flying today?" We have to wait for the weather to be right, with very little wind. When I am up in the air and gaze down at the landscape and see the horizon, that experience imparts real healing for me. The other benefit is that I have a friend who likes the same thing.

Here is the message: sometimes you have to include others. Establish new hobbies even during difficult times. What do you enjoy doing that could be done with friends? Make the effort so your time isn't spent wishing things were different. The Lord has a plan for our lives. If we are available to Him, new areas of fulfillment may emerge. Is there a need you can satisfy? What is God entrusting you with? How will He enable you to do that?

There are also times just to be. It's important to take advantage of those times when it's just about you learning to be and not necessarily having to do. Take time for yourself.

What special projects would you like to pursue? Big ones, small ones . . . just something. After our parents died in such quick succession (they lived in different parts of the country and all succumbed under different circumstances), we ended up with boxes of stuff. When parents are older, they downsize and downsize again, so mostly we had pictures. We went through stacks of pictures and organized them. Now we know what's in the boxes. It was a tender experience of seeing what was preserved of our memories. We know which photographs and things are especially precious that we will want to look back at from time to time. This effort also offered a certain kind of healing. Sometimes that happens in unexpected ways.

One opportunity for blessing came my way when I (Beth) picked up the church bulletin and saw an announcement for an outreach to international women; ladies who had moved to our area from all across the globe. I was newly retired from education and was curious about what they were going to do as outreach. When I went, I learned one of the things they offered was classes in English as a second language. I thought, "I can help with that," because I had been an English teacher.

I continued to go to the classes and tried some other things. The church hosts, a big event every month, part social, part inspirational, and part potluck with international foods. They also usually have a craft project the women do together each time. When we sit side by side trying to work with our hands, a spark of creativity emerges, which is good for our spirits. We look at each other's work, and maybe help, and also laugh at our own attempts, which we share with each other. This is how I learned to love creating relationships with international women.

In the midst of that, God said, "Now you're going overseas." God has sent us overseas a couple of times for ministry. Often it's not comfortable, but we love it. We love that God is there. He has work to do where He sends us and allows us to be involved. Be open to unexpected things. You never know what direction God will lead or where opportunities may come from.

If you attend any of our speaking engagements you will find books on a back table. That is another thing that we didn't plan, but God helped us realize there was a need for certain materials that we couldn't find in bookstores or online. So we started to sit with the Lord and work on some ideas we were having. "Can we do this together? You know we have never done this before," we asked the Lord. In three years, we produced three resources—only with the Lord.

We started with a grief resource for families with children who have lost a parent, like our grandson has. We wanted to give our only grandson answers to who God is in this part of life and how He has a plan for all of us. The resource answers several honest questions around the loss of a significant person in our lives. It's also a Bible study that delves deeper into each concept when more discussion is needed. We were looking for something to put into the hands of a child and others in the family to help foster honest discussion and bonding during devastating circumstances. God has used that book to help other families including those in the military.

It's a very personal tool for developing intimacy with the I Am in the context of suffering (as is the premise of Beth's book titled *I Am*). I've been given the privilege of partnering with a national organization to teach this in prisons as a small-group discipleship study for inmates who are eligible for release. It humbles me to see how God uses this approach to draw people out and be vulnerable in each other's presence.

As a side note, I (Beth) must mention that two of my favorite authors didn't write until tragedy struck and altered their lives. Catherine Marshall and Elisabeth Elliot took up the call to proclaim God's grace, and they showed by their very lives that there is life and purpose after loss. Both testify to the ways God brought support to them to fulfill their assignments and impact the world.

ACTIVITY 5

Think about how God is expanding your life and service as a result of loss. What new awareness have you developed? Trace how this awareness has developed.

How can you give God the glory in what you do? How has He used you to be a light in a dark world? How does He want to make you a powerful force in darkness?

5

REACHING THE HEART

Music is meaningful to me, and I (Beth) am finding the same to be true for other people as well. When I'm in a church service during the worship time, I often write the lyrics in my notebook. These thoughts minister truth to me and I want to meditate on the words.

What is it about the combination of sounds and words as symbols that communicate on a different plane from other forms of expression? It must have something to do the very makeup of our being. It's as if our Creator has placed within us melodies and rhythms that resonate with other parts of creation.

Instrumental pieces hold power over me as well. I've always loved movie soundtracks and their predecessor, tone poems. While driving during my usual weekly errands, I'll listen to a classical station on the radio. I don't welcome more chatter in my life, so these prolonged periods of pure lyrical sound ease my day.

Every now and again a selection will capture my attention, which requires me to pull over and write down its name for later, to see if I can order a copy online. Some songs seem timeless. Their messages convey eternity to my soul, and I want to be reminded of eternity.

ACTIVITY 6

Think about some of those songs and hymns that reach into your own heart, especially those that minister when only music can express what you're feeling, what someone else expresses are the very thoughts you couldn't find words for on your own. Write some of the lyrics or phrases that speak for you. When was the last time this happened? Why do you think this is so powerful?

We experienced the power of music in a particularly meaningful way when we attended an annual conference that provides gifted Bible teachers and incredible music. We listened to a singer from Wales, a humble man who went through a dramatic period of loss. His life came crashing down after he'd experienced a large degree of success but the Lord brought him up again. He now sings a song he didn't write, but which speaks deep truth to him, called "Healer of my Heart":

God of light, take away the dark of night.

Fill me with Your pure delight.

Touch me with Your hand,

God of Grace, flow into this lowly place.

Listen while Your children pray, Take me as I am.

Healer of my heart, lover of my soul,

Maker of the stars, the earth, the sky.

Come and make me whole.

Savior of this world, my voice praises You alone.

Healer of my heart, lover of my soul.

Immanuel, lead me to the deepest well.

Where never ending love prevails,

Drinking from Your cup. Prince of peace,

Forever live inside of me, keeper of eternity,

O Lord, revive me with Your touch.

Healer of my heart, lover of my soul,

Maker of the stars, the earth, the sky,

Come and make me whole.

Savior of this world, my voice praises You alone.

Healer of my heart, lover of my soul.[1]

I (Dave) listened to it over and over again and let it wash over me in soothing waves. Songs can do that. I am sure you have songs that do that for you. So don't forget the music. Sometimes when we go through loss, we lose the music.

Once, I (Beth) attended a discipleship group that met Saturday mornings. We chose different topics for about three years. Once, we studied a book called *Calm My Anxious Heart* by Linda Dillow. During this time, we realized there is music out there that helps us.

A lot of us in this group were facing health crises, while others were dealing with broken relationships or financial problems. All of us were walking with brokenness in one form or another. During this time, I found some powerfully challenging poems on brokenness from Amy Carmichael, a missionary to India. She wrote:

Hast thou no scar?

No hidden scar on foot, or side, or hand?

I hear thee sung as mighty in the land,

I hear them hail thy bright, ascendant star,

Hast thou no scar?

Hast thou no wound?

Yet I was wounded by the archers; spent,

Leaned Me against a tree to die; and rent

By ravening beasts that compassed Me, I swooned.

Hast thou no wound?

No wound? No scar?

Yet, as the Master shall the servant be,

And piercèd are the feet that follow Me;

But thine are whole; can he have followed far

Who hast nor wound nor scar?[2]

We also brought hymns and choruses for our time together. Sometimes we'd sing Stuart Townsend's choruses. One of his choruses is "In Christ Alone."

In Christ alone my hope is found.

He is my light, my strength, my song,

This Cornerstone, this solid ground,

Firm through the fiercest drought and storm.

What heights of love, what depths of peace,
When fears are stilled, when strivings cease.
My Comforter, my All in All,
Here in the love of Christ I stand.[3]

Stuart Townsend is a modern songwriter who loves hymns. He tries to bridge the gap between choruses and hymns, and his words, as a result, are vivid and memorable.

Perhaps music touches us so deeply because it lifts our spirits and penetrates into our souls as it refreshes or reminds us of truths we intuitively know. Its transcendent effect captures our minds and thrills our hearts unlike most other things. Music can bring healing in the midst of loss when we tend to misplace fundamental realities.

In loss we need ways to remember God's love for us. Though we may hear those words in a song or even Scripture, do we believe it? God's Word says this in a myriad of ways and in innumerable places. How do we miss that, and do we apply it in the situations we face? Our answer will determine our thoughts, our feelings, and the actions we take.

It's vital that we tell God when we don't feel loved by Him or others. If we don't take this step and tell Him about it, we will try to compensate for those deficits by manipulating others, holding grudges, avoiding people, or envying others' situations. We behave in these ways when we don't believe—at the heart level—that God and others love us.

The Scriptures also say Satan feeds us lies. He is the Father of Lies, the destroyer, the one who wants nothing good for us. Consequently, he carefully plants harmful thoughts in our minds. Sometimes they come through our imagination. We may think, "He looked at me funny. I bet I have a problem." We mentally work this whole scenario out until we are convinced there is something wrong with us and are miserable.

We must learn to operate on fact, not imagination or supposition. For instance, if you are waiting on results from a medical test, don't let your imagination take over and expect the worst. Wait until you get the facts.

The Enemy loves for us to feel unloved. He knows that in loss we're vulnerable to such feelings. He tells us things like, "They really don't care"; "You're not important enough to bother with"; or "You're too much trouble."

Oftentimes, what we are actually seeing in other people's behaviors, the ones that disappoint us, is that they don't know how to respond. They simply don't have the skills, or maybe they are, in fact, really busy. It's also possible they might simply be inadequate and ill-equipped to help.

Because of our own human fallibility and because we have disappointed people, the Enemy sets us up to respond out of hurt or fear. That is not a good place to stay.

Instead, recall some promises in Scripture that yank out a lie at its root. What do we know regardless of painful feelings? How has God revealed His heart to us and promised to provide for each need we will ever face? Can God fail to perform His promises? What do we know about His character? The more we know about God's character, the more faith we will be able to appropriate. This will sustain us.

Hebrews 13:8 says, "Jesus Christ is the same yesterday and today and forever." We all need someone who will be the same each day, someone dependable, not moody or fickle, who has all the love for us we can ever hope to experience.

First John 4:18 says, "Perfect love casts out fear." There are times when we're tempted to be afraid rather than trust in things we cannot understand or control. When you're uneasy and uncomfortable, repeat this verse to yourself. Bring the Lord into your fear and acknowledge His control. Because of what you know of God's character and ways, you can allow yourself to turn to Him with your feelings.

Ephesians 6:10–13 is a good Scripture passage to review when facing temptations based on feelings: "Finally, be strong in the Lord and in the strength of His might. Put on the full armor of God, so that you will be able to stand firm against the schemes of the devil. For our struggle is not against flesh and blood, but against the rulers, against the powers, against the world forces of this darkness, against the spiritual forces of wickedness in the heavenly places. Therefore, take up the full armor of God, so that you will be able to resist in the evil day, and having done everything, to stand firm."

Spiritual warfare is real. Who is your Enemy? Not your spouse, sibling, or coworker. But there is an Enemy who is very real and powerful. Ephesians 6 describes this Enemy when it says we are not dealing with flesh and blood but with those principalities and powers that are in place within a fallen world. Yet we have weapons God has given us so we can fight and defend against these enemies. We can stand in Christ.

Psalm 23 is also a wonderful passage to review for perspective and reassurance. Also, the Lord's Prayer, when repeated thoughtfully, reminds us who we are in relation to our Father.

We must ask ourselves, "Who is God, and who am I in relation to Him?" Ephesians 3:11–20 helps us put together a response to those questions.

I (Beth) made the decision a couple years ago, when faced with a trial that wouldn't go away that I wouldn't dwell there. I didn't want to let that be my sole focus. It would distract me from all the good God wanted for me, so I asked the Lord, "Help me with this trial that could crush me under its weight if I let it, and show me how not to dwell here." I learned, instead, how to dwell in Christ, to live in the land with Him, according to the promise. I let Him dwell in my heart, through faith, in order that I could be rooted and grounded in love. The caveat is, we must let Him dwell in our hearts by His Word and very presence.

Have you fully realized that life is a battle? But we can stand in His strength. Sometimes that is all that is required of us, to just stand. Christ is fighting the battle. Christ won the victory against the Enemy, which guarantees our position with Him. We would be outnumbered and overrun if we didn't have Him. The odds would be against us, but now we have "boldness and confident access" (Eph. 3:12).

Hebrews contains another encouraging word: "Let us hold fast the confession of our hope without wavering, for He who promised is faithful" (10:23). Even when we're not faithful, He is. We can be messes, not even able to focus, and our God will never desert us. And His plans won't fail.

PERSONAL REFLECTION

Excavate: deepening our roots. Read 2 Corinthians 4:10–12; Romans 8:1–2; and 2 Timothy 2:13.

Extend: branching out. What is the condition to having the life of Jesus manifested in us? How are we freed to live in the Spirit of life and not to be condemned? Does God expect perfection on our part?

Emerge: looking ahead. What is God saying to you about this? What will you do? As you look for this, how did you see this in action in your heart or life? (Provide an example and the date.)

Reaching our hearts is a work for a loving God to accomplish. After loss our hearts are wounded and He has to recover us at that heart level. There are many ways He accomplishes this. He knows us inside and out. His Word says His Spirit searches our hearts, knows our thoughts from afar, and never loses sight of us.

The psalms of David were his songs that attested to an intimate relationship with his Lord. Their art is in their beauty, raw emotion, honest expression of yearnings, and worship. David's songs have been our songs, too, especially when he responded to his loss. When we can't put words to our feelings, David's words are often our "lost chord."

Adelaide A. Proctor presents this idea in her poem "The Lost Chord":

Seated one day at the organ, I was weary and ill at ease,
And my fingers wandered idly over the noisy keys.
I know not what I was playing, or what I was dreaming then,
But I struck one chord of music like the sound of a great Amen."[4]

NOTES

1. Huw Priday, "Healer of My Heart," Priday Productions, 2008. Used by permission.

2. Amy Carmichael, "No Scar?" *Toward Jerusalem* (Fort Washington, PA: CLC Publications, 1936), 85.

3. Stuart Townsend, "In Christ Alone," Thankyou Music (PRS), Capitol-CMGPublishing.com, 2002. Used by permission.

4. Adelaide Proctor, "The Lost Chord," in *The Pocket Book of Quotations*, ed. Henry Davidoff (New York: Pocket, 1952).

6

STAYING SOFT

Jill Briscoe, a creative and insightful Bible teacher, wrote a book about finishing well called *Faith Enough to Finish*.[1] She said that people get life and God mixed up. What struck us by that concept was that life hurts and has things we don't want to deal with, but that is life, not God. That's why we shouldn't blame God when life hurts.

We live in a fallen world, which means we will experience loss in many forms. We see this each day all around us. Warped values, selfishness, unplanned events, and unfair practices all seem to victimize us. The consequences and pain of those things aren't reflective of God, they're the result of the sin-filled world we live in.

Living authentically as the redeemed in this fallen world means that we will respond not to those things but to the truth that comes from the Creator of the universe. We don't look at media examples or opinion polls. Instead we ask, "What do we know that never changes? How do we know it? What's its source?" That is what we need to pay attention to.

From the time we lived in Northern California we've known a special couple. Serving together at a church known for Bible teaching that applies to life, we were aware of how God blessed that ministry with far-reaching impact because they proclaimed His truth and expected the Holy Spirit to make it real in all our lives. This calling wasn't without opposition though.

Our friends, Greg and Bonnie, were anticipating being new parents when they lost two babies, one right after the other. It was revealed that a rare genetic defect was responsible. Their first baby, a darling little boy who lacked the right enzyme to metabolize his food, died within days of his birth. That was very hard. Then Bonnie got pregnant again very soon, and nine months later they had a precious baby girl who was expected to be healthy but soon was diagnosed with the same disorder. That young couple was stunned and brokenhearted but continued in ministry.

About forty years later, when our son was killed in Iraq, I (Beth) saw those same friends while visiting family in California. We had breakfast at a restaurant one morning with their grandson—because you know what?—God gave them more children. They adopted Kaitlin, who was an answer to the prayers of many who knew them. Within two weeks after their second child died, someone in the church said, "Let's pray for a baby for this couple." Someone in that same service was pregnant and needed to place her baby with a godly couple who could care for it. That baby was Kaitlin, and their grandson is her third child.

That morning when I was having breakfast with them in the aftermath of our loss, Greg said, "There's reality, and then there are God's promises; and the challenge is to bring those two things together. You can look at reality and see this is what is, and then see God's promises—these things are sure, and these things will happen."

How do you bring those two things together? God knows and you can ask Him how to do that. It's a process.

PERSONAL REFLECTION

Excavate: deepening our roots. Read John 15:18–21; 17:11–18; and 2 Timothy 1:12; 3:1–17.

Extend: branching out. What did Jesus ask the Father to do for us before He went to the cross? What does Jesus say we can expect from the world? What kinds of difficulty will come in the last days? How are we equipped to handle it? From what do we derive our confidence?

Emerge: looking ahead. What is God saying to you about this? What will you do? As you look for this, how did you see this in action in your heart or life? (Provide an example and the date.)

One of the things that helps with integrating God's promises into our losses is staying soft. Life can harden us. Loss can harden us. We need to ask the Lord to keep us soft so this won't occur because if that happens, we will be less and less able to receive the grace God wants to give us. The Holy Spirit won't have access to do His work or to permeate our souls.

How does hardness happen? Entitlement. Sometimes we feel entitled to hold on to our feelings. We feel justified in this, because "They hurt me, and they are still hurting me." We withhold ourselves from God, even though He is the lover of our souls and the healer of our hearts, and we refuse to forgive. In Mark 10:2–5, the

Pharisees were testing Jesus on the sensitive subject of divorce and God's plan. Jesus referred them to Moses and the law, which introduced the concept "because of your hardness of heart" (v. 5).

I (Beth) did my own study this past year on forgiveness. In the wake of some of our losses, I wanted to know what the Bible said about it. I read a couple of books on the subject, which were very helpful. I also found some important things in Scripture that talk about forgiveness and what that process looks like in different situations. Forgiveness has to be cultivated and become a habit. It has to be something we get really good at, without resentment, because there are lots of different levels on which we have to use it. We can't do it just one time, especially when "they" do the same thing again. Marriage is like this. Dave and I are still married because we can forgive over and over. Human beings require this. Christ knew this when He suffered rejection and betrayal. His own life guaranteed forgiveness without limits, and He gives His life for our wholeness in the midst of the ache of rejection or the fury of betrayal.

By staying soft we allow what God allows. When I was studying the topic of revival a few years ago, God gave me the phrase "Allow what God allows." Can I allow what He allows? Can I trust in His resources to keep walking in truth? That is the challenge: Can we keep walking in truth, despite the hurt? He will guide us. He will give us rest. He will honor our cries for help. He will cause us to stand. Becoming hard only short-circuits that blessed "way of escape" (1 Cor. 10:13). This is how we experience the freedom Christ died to give us.

Romans 12:14–18 tells us how to handle relationships that are tough. It says, "Bless those who persecute you; bless and do not curse. Rejoice with those who rejoice, and weep with those who weep. Be of the same mind toward one another; do not be haughty in mind, but associate with the lowly. Do not be wise in your own estimation. Never pay back evil for evil to anyone. Respect what is right in the sight of all men. If possible, so far as it depends on you, be at peace with all men." This also will keep you soft.

Another Scripture passage to meditate on is Psalm 22. This psalm is an odd mixture of an anguished cry and a song of praise. Someone was hurt deeply and yet found reason to praise at the same time. He felt the pain while believing the truth that never changes. Ephesians 4:17–27 is another passage of encouragement to stay soft.

The Devil is waiting for you. He will take advantage of you, and you will be the loser when he does. Therefore, lay aside all that entangles you, and don't give Satan the opportunity. The Word is the help you need for your heart to stay soft.

Have you been the recipient of another's meanness? Have you been mean? Being mean is when you hurt someone because of your own woundedness. When people are mean, we must learn to view it from the bigger picture that it's about them and God. There's something unresolved in that relationship.

So don't let life calcify you. Don't let those layers build up, because God will have to chip away the layers, and that will be an unpleasant and slow process. It is also unnecessary. Life doesn't have to harden us; rather, it can make us stronger. It also can make us more beautiful and loving, especially if we've suffered. When we allow Jesus to live His life in us, in all of life's dimensions, we will reflect Him. When others see us, they will see Him.

ACTIVITY 7

This activity is about the four parts of prayer, a vital component to staying soft. First, we confess, which means that we agree with God in regard to areas that need His work in our lives. We listen as He speaks truth, hard as it may be to hear. Let Him reassure you that He is still in control. He knows all about it and is working in spite of the lack of evidence you can't see. He is still working. At times He may give us glimpses, but our vision is so limited compared to His.

Second, we praise Him for who He is, not for what He can give. Staying soft requires surrender and submission. Surrender is giving it back to Him, a supernatural response, something human beings can't do by themselves.

Third, we ask for His will to be done, even if it's not our will (see Matt. 26:38–42). When we heard about our other son's car accident, we knew it was bad. The hospital chaplain would not tell us how he was doing. We just had to get in the car and head to the hospital. We live twenty-five minutes from the hospital, and as we were driving, I sensed the Holy Spirit say, "Let me have it." So I (Beth) prayed while Dave drove. I prayed for our son, and I prayed that God's will be done. Because I didn't know the big picture, I didn't know what God had in mind. To pray that prayer is not a natural response.

Last, we thank Him that He is able. Thank Him that He is able to do any of these things we are bringing to Him, especially the impossible. His character is key. So is learning to be content, to rest. Hebrews 13:5–6 provides a guide: "Make sure that your character is free from the love of money, being content with what you have; for He himself has said, 'I will never desert you, nor will I ever forsake you,' so that we confidently say, 'the LORD is my helper, I will not be afraid. What will man do to me?'" And Hebrews 12:15 warns, "See to it that no one comes short of the grace of God; that no root of bitterness springing up causes trouble, and by it many be defiled."

Take time now to write out your own prayer.

Confess, praise, ask, and thank—all parts of talking intimately with the Lord in our times of need. Using this prayer format will aid you as we move forward together.

A woman recently attended our "How to LIVE with a Broken Heart" workshop and stated that she was a professional in the people-helping field and was there to get background. She needed to learn our approach so she could more effectively assist people who were living with loss. At the end of the workshop, she approached me (Dave) and told me that she was so thankful she came. She had come not thinking she had anything to grieve or work on, but as she went through the journaling activities, she came face-to-face with some long-lasting losses in her life that the Lord wanted to address.

We have become more resolute in our belief that we need to take a long look at, evaluate, and think through the losses we are living with so God has access to them. He will meet us there.

NOTE

1. Jill Briscoe, *Faith Enough to Finish* (Carol Stream, IL: Tyndale, 2001), 10.

7
HARD-WON INSIGHTS

When we were first asked to offer an elective workshop at a
Bible conference we respected, the organizers, aware of our story,
specifically asked us to make our topic about loss. At the time, we
hadn't collected our thoughts, but we soon realized the Lord was
feeding us ideas and helping us organize principles that could help
others trying to navigate the same choppy waters we'd faced.

We sat in our living room with an empty notebook in an attempt
to answer the question, "What have we been learning the past couple
of years that could help someone else?" We didn't know yet, however,
that we were merely in the middle of a whole series of losses that
God would allow us to experience.

What follows in the next few chapters is the fruit of our ardent
study of daily life and the God who walks with us, not merely a
rehash of other popular or academic sources. Testing these concepts
came at great personal expense: our suffering and crying out to our
Lord for His wisdom and mercy to grow and learn, not hunker down

and simply endure the buffeting and battering of repeated trials. What we offer is what we know works, and it's our privilege to share it with those wanting answers and help. There is no particular order to these tips. All are equally important for life during and after losses. So with that in mind, here are some hard-won insights learned through submission.

STAY IN THE WORD—IT WILL RENEW PERSPECTIVE

Look for God's character and draw strength from the examples of other desperate people (see Rom. 15:4). The Bible is full of them. Psalm 119 clarifies the quality and the influence the Word of God has: "Your word is a lamp to my feet and a light to my path" (v. 105).

At the end of the camping season, we were camped at the North Rim of the Grand Canyon. We, along with several others, were watching the sun sink ever lower on the horizon on a cool, fall evening at the historic lodge. After dinner and a talk by one of the rangers, we returned to our campsite later than expected. The fabulous night sky was upon us and all we had for the walk back was a cell phone. Once on the path, we flipped open the cell phone for small doses of light to keep us on the trail. Unless we had light, though in smaller amounts than we would have preferred, there was no way to find our way.

This is exactly what the Word of God does. It gives us direction and keeps us walking the right way. Read the Bible for yourself and we're sure you'll agree. It truly is a light for your life. Simply said, you'll receive insight to guide you (see Phil. 2:16).

Another verse in Psalm 119 concerning the quality of the Scriptures is verse 107: "I am severely afflicted; give me life, O LORD, according to your word!" (ESV). Life comes from His Word. As this verse implies, the Word revives us. We can breathe again. What can we do that will allow the Word of God to have priority?

Our Lord is not necessarily saying He will take away the affliction but that He will help us to be fully alive, though in it. We will be restored as we meditate on God's Word. Real life happens when we truly understand what the Word is saying in our circumstances. Are you reading the Word and applying it to your life? Are you making it real? Reading the Word is your connection to God. Please, do it for your recovery.

"You are my hiding place and my shield; I hope in your word" (v. 114 ESV). The Word provides a place where we can hide, and we are covered by it. The Word is a shelter. It's a place to go and be safe. We have hope because the Word has answers to our concerns and fears.

We can hide in the Word when we need to retreat from the pain of this life. Psalm 119:114 also states that the Word is a shield, which can be used both defensively and offensively. We can attack the feelings we have with the Word. We can strike out, as well as be kept safe, with this shield. As we immerse ourselves in it, this is what the Word does in our lives.

The same chapter describes a provision of God we all need: "Uphold me according to your promise, that I may live, and let me not be put to shame in my hope!" (v. 116 ESV). We are upheld and sustained. We can lean on what God says and have a full life in Christ because of the Word. The Word of God gives us insight, revives us, serves as a hiding place or a shelter, and sustains us.

I (Dave) experienced this firsthand. When we were informed about the death of our son serving in Iraq, we were in Temple,

Texas, near Fort Hood, visiting our daughter-in-law and grandson. Almost immediately, I realized I needed to get back to Colorado Springs, where our home is, to tell our other son and my father this news in person. Within hours I boarded a plane at the airport on Fort Hood. That flight carried a large contingent of army personnel. As I saw those men and women in uniform, all I could think of was Ian and our loss.

I cried almost to the point of sobbing. Then the Lord gently encouraged me to open the small Bible I had taken on our trip to Texas. As I read, the Word of God washed over me. For the first time in those tumultuous hours, I felt safe.

The Word, which is so alive, was sustaining me. In troubling experiences, the Word has become a friend to us like it never has before. Since that day, I look forward, in a new way, to my time in the Word. Are there days when I don't look at the Word? Sure, but I can honestly say that I feel like I have missed being with a close friend. It always gives me guidance and comfort. Our urgent plea to you is to read, study, and then make the Word your own.

PRAY HONESTLY AT ALL TIMES—NO HIDING, NO POSTURING

Give the Father all that weighs you down; open your heart to the best friend you'll ever know. He will not judge you; He will listen (see 1 Sam. 1:10–11, 15–16; 2:1–9).

Jesus is our example for this truth. When Jesus prayed, He didn't hide. He didn't posture—He did not remind the Father that He was the Son of God. Instead, He revealed His pain, desires, and needs to the Father and knew the Father would not judge Him. He was safe to tell all He was thinking and feeling (see, for example, Matt. 26:36–44).

The cross loomed on the horizon in Jesus' life. He was sorrowful and troubled. He was "grieved and distressed" (v. 37). He was grieved unto death. This was the real thing. This was deep loss. The question is, how did He approach God in prayer? First of all, He called Him "Father" (v. 39). He knew Him intimately. Second, Jesus expressed His deepest emotion. He simply said, "Take the cross away." Third, He finished His prayer by saying, "It is all up to You, Father. I will do what You want Me to do, because I know Your plans are best. I trust You."

Now take a moment to look at the disciples and how they responded in their moment of deep concern. They were probably thinking back to the evening they'd just spent with Jesus in the upper room. Maybe Peter was mulling over what the Lord had told him concerning his denial. "When could that happen? I would never deny my Lord," he might have thought.

Then John possibly wondered about some of the other statements Jesus had made. "What about this Spirit that will fill me? But the requirement was that Jesus has to go away. . . . Where would He go?"

James may have sat there not knowing what he was watching for. "Could something or someone be coming?" They probably didn't get to the point of praying much. Too much to take in. It was easier to fall asleep after such events rather than pray.

What about us? Do we sleep, or do we pray? Really pray and empty our hearts with our best Friend? What kind of a relationship do we have with the Father? Do we fall on our faces before Him?

Consider the possibility that we might not pray as we should. Praying honestly at all times demonstrates dependence rather than independence. That's a position to value. When the Spirit points to a need or when you're overwhelmed by circumstances, pray without hesitation, and stay at it until you sense there's nothing more to say. Then make sure you've been listening for a response.

FEEL THE PAIN—LET THE SPIRIT MINISTER

Ministering is the Spirit's role and the reason He lives within. We have to feel the pain rather than avoid it or cover it up for Him to help us. Let yourself cry and ask the Holy Spirit to comfort, guide, and intercede when there are no words left to say. The Scriptures are very clear that God's Spirit is present to support us when we do: "Likewise, the Spirit helps us in our weakness. For we do not know what to pray for as we ought, but the Spirit himself intercedes for us with groanings too deep for words. And he who searches hearts knows what is the mind of the Spirit, because the Spirit intercedes for the saints according to the will of God" (Rom. 8:26–27 ESV).

We often don't know what to pray when we're in pain. The Holy Spirit speaks for us with groanings to the Father. What intimacy we have with the Spirit. He gets us. He understands and doesn't try to correct us. It's all acceptable.

Second Corinthians 1:3–5 says that in all our afflictions we'll receive comfort from the "Father of mercies." It further states, "Just as the sufferings of Christ are ours in abundance, so also our comfort is abundant through Christ"—so much so, we can even comfort others who need it.

First Peter acknowledges anxieties and notes their source. Issues in our lives, when mismanaged, can create worry. "Casting all your anxiety on Him, because He cares for you" is a better way to deal with pain (1 Pet. 5:7). How do we avoid feeling the pain and inadvertently miss receiving this help from God? We keep busy. We self-medicate — anything from alcohol and drugs to shopping and sex. So what should we do when pain comes?

An example from our life comes from a regular routine we've developed. We work out at a recreation center across town, and most of the time we ride together. One day, however, we had different places to go after our workout and drove separate vehicles. After swimming, I (Dave) headed down the road to run some errands and drove past a place I've gone past maybe fifty times since Ian went home to be with the Lord. But this time was different.

I glanced at a group of cabins placed in a grove of tall pine trees, and it hit me that this was the place I used to drop off Ian for his first job. Out of nowhere, I responded with tremendous emotion, and I just kept going. I probably was speeding as I tried to get away from a memory that now created sorrow. I found myself pulling over, though, and turning around to drive back. I pulled into the compound and got out to walk around the property. I felt all the pain associated with that memory. After I completed that time with the Lord, the memory grew sweet again. It was a special time with my son that I can once again treasure for the rest of my life.

What about you? Are you avoiding pain that comes from living life? This pain can come at any time. You can be sitting reading the paper and a thought suddenly overwhelms you. You can be at a favorite restaurant, and because it's associated with a portion of your loss, this experience becomes highly emotional. What is it for you? When this happens, make sure you allow yourself to feel the pain and hear the Lord in it. Allow your heavenly Father to love and comfort you. The vital part is to include the Lord in the process. Nothing gets healed if the Lord is not involved.

BE GOOD TO YOURSELF

Take care of yourself by exercising (it will lift your mood and give you endurance), getting sleep and rest when you get tired, eating nutritious meals, and making time for fun with friends who accept you "as is."

When you go through loss, there's a tendency to ignore taking care of yourself. Make sure you have a plan that includes exercise. Exercise classes, in particular, accomplish two things: first, they get you moving and strengthen you for the life ahead; and second, exercising with others is often more fun.

The other part of taking care of yourself is being with friends who accept you as you are. Kris and Brett are two friends who accept us in this way. They invite us to different activities with no strings attached. Kris called recently and asked if we wanted to go to a hockey game with them. The hockey was really great, but the best part was being with people who honestly love us and have no requirements for us. They let us be who we are, pain and all.

READ INSPIRATIONAL BOOKS OR TAKE A CLASS

There are other worthwhile books, in addition to the Bible, that inspire. What's an interest of yours? Read about that. Recently, I (Dave) developed an interest in beekeeping and have been on my computer reading and thinking about the possibility of being a bee-keeper. It's fun to open the door to new interests. What do you want to learn about? There are probably materials or classes that address your desire.

Take classes that provide helpful information, social contacts, or develop new skills. We have taken a variety of classes together and separately. We're what some call lifelong learners. One class we really enjoy learning together is Zumba, the Latin dance and exercise class. We found out about it at our fairly progressive senior center and were able to meet some great people while brushing up on our dance steps. I (Beth) also enjoy taking art classes at various venues around town and making time for creativity and being with others who want to stretch themselves.

BE ARMED TO STAND IN THE FACE OF THE ENEMY'S ATTACKS

Loss makes us vulnerable and our Enemy will take advantage of this. Satan knows that when you are going through suffering and dealing with loss that you are on the threshold of opportunity. This opportunity is showing people in your life that you are dependent on Jesus and Jesus alone. You love Him and are willing to follow Him, especially now. If Satan can eliminate this ministry (and it is a ministry), he's gained a victory. Therefore, be prepared for spiritual warfare.

Ephesians 6:10–13 describes how we approach this enemy and the warfare he brings. When this passage says we are to "put on the full armor of God" (v. 11), it's a warning that we need to be prepared. We need God's armor and should not approach Satan in our own strength, which is impotent compared to Satan's power. By using God's spiritual power, represented in these pieces of armor, we can stand against the Devil's devices. Satan will use any ruthless method to destroy us physically, emotionally, and spiritually.

We once visited a castle and saw medieval armor, which was obviously designed to protect all the vital body parts. Our spiritual armor likewise protects us vitally while enabling us to stand and obtain victory in Christ.

Another truth revealed in this passage is what we war against. "We struggle not against flesh and blood" (v. 12). Yet doesn't it seem like our problems are with people? We find out people are speaking against us. Maybe people have done wrong and hurtful things to us. But here Scripture says that our real enemies are not mere people but "the rulers . . . the powers . . . the world forces of this present darkness . . . the spiritual forces of wickedness in the heavenly places" (v. 12). It's clear we war against demonic beings who want to destroy us. And yes, they at times use people.

This perspective gives us an understanding of the warfare we are involved with every day of our lives and of who is attacking us. Stand with Jesus, firm in His power. He will take care of you in the battle.

First Peter 5:8–9 explains the approach of Satan's attack: "Be sober-minded; be watchful. Your adversary the devil prowls around like a roaring lion, seeking someone to devour. Resist him, firm in your faith, knowing that the same kinds of suffering are being experienced by your brotherhood throughout the world" (ESV).

Three words stand out concerning Satan's approach when attacking people. He *prowls*, he *roars*, and he *seeks*. A number of years ago at our local zoo, we were standing at a cage containing a pride of mountain lions. Some lay on rocks and others lounged in trees unconcerned about any of us. Yet as we watched them, a little boy ran by and every animal stood up, crouched down, and prepared to attack. It was frightening. Thank God for the cage that separated them from this defenseless little boy.

Those mountain lions did exactly what Satan does. He can perceive and will take advantage of any weakness we have. He prowls around wanting to devour his prey. Are we easy prey, or do we have a cage between us and Satan—Jesus Christ and His armor? Stay engaged with Christ.

Though we've made a good start at defining and utilizing survival strategies during and after loss, there are several more tips to consider. Ask God to show you how He will aid you in making changes and in appropriating more of those things He's made available to bring hope and healing when life is distressing. He is near.

8

DIVINE VISION

Hope is proactive, never passive. It's what we gain when we understand its source. Hope is bound up in our identities as children of the living God. What we are called to after making that life-changing decision to follow Christ affects every decision after that. New realities are at work in us that need expression. Following Christ opens a door previously unseen but now within our grasp.

FIND YOUR CALLING, YOUR HEART, AND LIVE FROM PURPOSE EACH DAY

God wants to use your gifts and talents, along with your newfound compassion, to build the kingdom (see 1 Cor. 15:10).

Has there been ministry in your life because of your loss? Expect it. It might not be what you think of when you consider ministry. It might be one-on-one at Starbucks with someone you didn't even know before you walked in to get coffee. Be aware of divine appointments like this in your everyday life. God has plans for us in relation to others. Are we open to responding to these opportunities?

God has a purpose for all we are walking through. It is a paradox, really. Bad things have happened to us, yet God uses these same situations to mold us, strengthen us, and prepare us for a calling that is unique. I (Beth) don't know what this purpose or calling looks like for you, but I am becoming more aware of God's calling in my own life. However, sometimes I don't accept my calling in certain instances.

Most times I have a choice to make as I come in contact with someone: Will I be faithful to what God is calling me to at this moment? Along with that, each one of us has a unique cluster of spiritual gifts and complementary talents God has given us. We're simply asked to let Him develop them and put them into service.

There comes a time in loss in which we have to finally focus on something other than ourselves. This is where calling comes in. Rather than focusing on what other people say or think, concentrating on building the kingdom of God becomes more important. Sharing a purpose behind your loss and the grace and strength you have gained because God has touched you is now possible. Proclaiming the resurrected Christ by living life dependent on Him is the message everyone needs to see in practice. In loss God's Spirit can transform us by having the mind of Christ when we have shared in His sufferings.

As we respond to our unique calling after a life-changing experience, there often seems to be a sense of urgency. We want to be about the Lord's business for the time available to us. The command "Whatever your hand finds to do, do it with all your might" (Eccl. 9:10) resonates with our spirit. We are directed to work with a desire to finish the race and do it with everything in us, depending only on God and His leading. Colossians 3:23–24 continues this thought but also reminds us where our focus is as we reach out: "Whatever you do, work heartily, as for the Lord and not for men, knowing that from the Lord you will receive the inheritance as your reward. You are serving the Lord Christ" (ESV).

This calling, the work God gives, is to be done unto the Lord and not for men. I (Dave) would admit that this has been a glaring problem in my own life. I have cared too much what people think about me and my ministry. No longer.

Though in a different way, I (Beth) have also seen this tendency in the work environment. At times I edited my thoughts and held back because I sensed I was among a group hostile to a Christian point of view. Now, however, the losses we've lived through have purged this distorted, human leaning. God has given us freedom to do what He wants us to do, although He will periodically test this.

As opportunities present themselves, we may have to confront such fears all over again. Becoming more sensitive, we now check each other if we're aware of this habit reasserting itself. Self-monitoring works too. I (Dave) am learning instead to make a habit of praying, "What do You want me to do, Lord? I'll do that." What is God telling you to do? Whatever it is, it's about pleasing Him and Him alone.

WHAT IS SEEN IS TEMPORARY—WHAT IS UNSEEN IS ETERNAL

There really is a cloud of witnesses that cheers you on and wants to see you fight the good fight and finish well. Throw off everything, along with the sin, that hinders your race and fix your eyes on Jesus, not on your problems. Give your problems to Him.

Colossians 3:1–17 tells what life should be in Christ. What is real? What is important? What will last? What we are living with is truly temporary. Paul, in this passage, clarified reality. First, the question is, "Have you been raised up with Christ?" (see v. 1). In other words, have you accepted Christ as Savior? Is He the one you'll follow in this life? If that's the choice you've made, He'll give you His power to live effectively in all circumstances.

Paul also pointed out how we're to set our minds on what is "above" (v. 1). We're to put away the old life, which only looks to ourselves and our wants. When dealing with loss, it's necessary to see there actually is another reality—the eternal realm, where the resurrected Jesus sits with the Father in a position of authority. This is happening in real time, in our present as well as in our future. Eternity, not only the physical lives we live, is for now.

How do we do all this? It has something to do with our calling to put off the old self and all the flesh-feeding activities, and put on the new self, which is Christ himself.

How do we eliminate sin and foster change? Scripture says we turn to the Lord, in each instance, and let Him remove the offense. He removes any ingrained, self-serving tendency and puts on life, every time. Everything from our self prior to Christ can be thrown off. So finish well. Call sin what it is and put it to death. Turn to the Lord to replace those tendencies with renewed life, which is God's glorious image in you.

CONSIDER HIM OUR MODEL WHO ENDURED

Jesus, who endured such oppression from sinful men so that we might not grow weary and lose heart, is our model and our life. He has all authority over the Enemy and will defeat him and deliver you in His name.

Jesus is our model and our life. The way He was able to exist in this world is the way we are able to exist—through His power. Remember, it's always His power, which comes from the risen Christ in us, that gets us through to the end. We have the Holy Spirit dwelling within to accomplish His work in us. First Corinthians 15:24–26 echoes this idea: "Then comes the end, when he delivers the kingdom to God the Father after destroying every rule and every authority and power. For he must reign until he has put all his enemies under his feet. The last enemy to be destroyed is death" (ESV).

Do you hear the promise that Jesus is in control both now and ultimately? He will reign in each of our lives and protect us from our enemies. Our God is the key factor, not the troubling situation. He will reign.

Let's clarify something important: Whatever brought you to seek help with loss is an event, a difficult one, but it shouldn't be the overriding concept. Your loss is not the highest reality or all-defining truth in your life. Whatever is happening in or around you, as God's child, view Jesus as the model and the means. Keep your eyes faithfully trained on Him, regardless of the situation, though significant and painful. The biggest reality in your life is the fact that God rules and reigns. *That* is paramount.

Recently, I (Dave) had a wild week of spiritual attacks and decided to fly my powered parachute. This experience generally proves to be transforming for me. I prepared the night before by charging up the radio and loading the truck with all the gear. In the morning, I got up early and departed to a small airport.

Arriving around 6:30 a.m., I performed preflight inspections and started the engine, warming it up for about ten minutes. After carefully laying out the chute, I strapped in, did one more check of the instruments, released the brake, raised my feet onto the steering bars, and pushed the throttle forward. As the chute rose overhead and all the cells filled with air, I checked again to see if it was safe to take off before leaving the ground.

After traveling eight miles or so, I made a sweeping turn and headed west. The panorama of the Front Range of the Rocky Mountains came into immediate view. As I flew alone above the arid plains of ranchland, God's creation was right there before me. The snowcapped peaks of continuous mountain ranges from north to south, with Pikes Peak looming above the others.

As I settled down to perform some maneuvers and enjoy the flight, I glanced to my right and spied a hawk that had decided to accompany me. I couldn't believe it. I just kept flying straight ahead, for as long as the hawk stayed with me. After considerable time, he left, and I made my way back to the airport to land. My hobby had done what it needed to do. I was amazed all over again. For me, life has become all about God. After dealing with several attacks from the Enemy and questioning, "Why me? Why now?" I regained a glimpse of the living God and saw difficulties fade away. He became prominent again in my life.

Is He prominent in your life? If not, put yourself in a position to become amazed by His glory.

LOOK TO THE HORIZON AND RUN WITH ENDURANCE

Don't be afraid. The Lord is at your side, goes before you, and has your back (Isa. 52:12). We can endure because, like Christ, there's joy set before us.

This is evident in each of our lives. The Enemy wants to distract us, and at times we find ourselves somewhere out in left field doing something God didn't have planned for us. We sometimes find ourselves sidelined by circumstances or what someone says. We're tempted, and if we respond to those evil thoughts they could destroy us.

First John 4:4, 18 shows a different view of a life in Christ: "Little children, you are from God and have overcome them; for he who is in you is greater than he who is in the world. There is no fear in love, but perfect love casts out fear. For fear has to do with punishment, and whoever fears has not been perfected in love" (ESV).

According to these verses, we have overcome through the power of Jesus Christ. The Holy Spirit in you, John said, is much greater than any spirit in the world. Do you know God loves you? Do you acknowledge this only intellectually or deep down at the heart level? God says He loves you, repeatedly. So don't be afraid. When the Enemy wants to distract, derail, and destroy, meditate on this truth: The almighty power of a loving God dwells within you. When we allow His love to replace our fear, then it's possible we can look at the finish line. Fear disables this ability.

Paul talked realistically about the end of his race in 2 Timothy 4:6–7: "For I am already being poured out as a drink offering, and the time of my departure has come. I have fought the good fight, I have finished the race, I have kept the faith." What a great statement to be able to make as the end drew near. Paul saw the horizon ever closer and was finishing with endurance.

How do we live like Paul? Keep the faith and focus on the finish line. You race well when you can see Jesus waiting for you at the finish line.

Once I (Dave), a non-runner, was recruited by friends in my college dorm for an intramural track meet. They wanted me to run both the quarter- and half-mile races toward the end of the day. There were two problems with this: (1) I was really out of shape; and (2) I had never run track before in my life. A teammate approached me to ask what my strategy was to win the race.

I told him that my strategy was not to be last! It was obvious that I did not know much about racing. In the quarter mile, I placed fourth out of five. The half mile was next, and I was exhausted after the previous race. When the race was half over, I was second from the last. Not knowing how to run track, I found myself looking back, trying to see the last runner. When I did this, to my surprise, I found myself losing ground every time I turned my head. But instead, when I strained to see the finish line, I started to put yards between me and the last runner. As a result, I didn't finish last. And more importantly, I finished.

When we intently look to Christ and focus on the finish line, we win the race. Our race. Can bad things still happen to us? Absolutely. But when we concentrate on Christ, we will finish the race.

Can we experience losses and still win the race? Yes, without a doubt. The Scripture says that in Christ, we can suffer loss and still complete our course. Christ himself did. Many, if not all, of His followers did also.

Therefore, keep looking at the finish line. Concentrate on finishing well. Through reading and applying the Word, you'll be able to endure because you know what it says and what that means as you run your race. Then run with endurance and finish the race God has called you to. It's yours alone.

Divine vision, then, is about accepting our unique calling, knowing the difference between temporary and eternal things, having a model who shows the way, and looking to the horizon while planting each step as a conscious choice. What's next? Learning to possess the land along the way. The Father has given us the land and will show us how to live in it.

9

ENDURANCE TRAINING

The Israelites stood at the edge of the land God promised. There it lay, right in front of them, a gift from God just ready to be claimed. But when the spies' reports came back, they weren't so sure anymore. This fertile land, chosen by God, contained giants. Only Caleb and Joshua were in favor of proceeding with God's plan. The other ten spies told Moses and the people, "We are not able to go up against the people, for they are too strong for us" (Num. 13:31). That was enough to discourage the whole assembly. "And the people wept that night. All the sons of Israel grumbled against Moses and Aaron . . . 'Would it not be better for us to return to Egypt?'" (14:1–3). Not only did they question their leadership, they also questioned God's, and what followed was a detour of several decades of wilderness wandering before God would bring back the next generation.

Isn't that what we do when the Lord gives us a challenge? We listen to those voices designed to cause fear and discouragement. We fail to see God in the midst and only want to turn back. We can't go forward with Him unless we choose to. Yet the promises and purposes of God remain. Will we miss them? No, we can learn from this ancient example: Enter and possess the land! Yes, there are giants, but the Lord will fight for you in creative and miraculous ways. Let the Good Shepherd carry you, stay yoked with the Savior, and abide in the Vine while He produces the fruit. Your walk is important to others.

Our ministry, *by His design*, has a lean staff, just us and occasionally various others who join us for specific tasks. Because we came from work cultures that required staff meetings to share necessary information and to clarify duties, I (Beth) instituted our own version. I'm the structured one who thrives on knowing what's going on, and though Dave is a great administrator, he's more comfortable with doing his part while letting things flow. He'll tell you, though, how we've made these meetings beneficial and actually enjoyable at times. The secret is to appreciate our different approaches and be somewhere other than our house.

At one of our "staff meetings," I matter-of-factly said, "You know that you don't teach this thing about new life and possessing the land, right?" Then I blinked and realized that might be a little insensitive.

"Well," Dave said, "please explain that to me. What do you mean?"

With that opening, I went on. "When you have new life, it's like in the Old Testament when the children of Israel went into the Promised Land. They were called to 'possess the land,' to take it all. To possess what they had, possess what they were given. I'm called to possess what God has given me at this time and trust He will strengthen me to be faithful." More discussion ensued, and I was glad we had the chance to examine our personal positions and enhance mutual understanding in this crucial area.

I continue to look at this concept because I don't want to miss it. At various stages in my life, "possessing the land" has looked somewhat different, yet with certain commonalities. Its lessons, though, are specific to my walk at any given time.

During our conversation, Dave helped me when he explained, "When you look at the children of Israel and how they possessed the land, you realize they did not do it well." Dave saw "possessing the land" as a zigzag journey. Like us, the Israelites were faithful for a while, but they also allowed others to possess the land with them, a practice the Lord forbade in the instructions He gave to Moses. They disobeyed those instructions and began to be pulled away from their Lord and His promises.

We are called to possess the land and not allow giants to mingle in our relationship with God. Instead, we do battle and drive them out in God's power. "For everyone who has been born of God overcomes the world. And this is the victory that has overcome the world—our faith" (1 John 5:4 ESV).

By faith we possess the land. Faith enables us to possess what we are called to. Joshua 5:13–15 says,

When Joshua was by Jericho, he lifted up his eyes and looked, and behold, a man was standing before him with his drawn sword in his hand. And Joshua went to him and said to him, "Are you for us, or for our adversaries?" And he said, "No; but I am the commander of the army of the LORD. Now I have come." And Joshua fell on his face to the earth and worshiped and said to him, "What does my lord say to his servant?" And the commander of the LORD's army said to Joshua, "Take off your sandals from your feet, for the place where you are standing is holy." And Joshua did so. (ESV)

When Joshua encountered the man with a drawn sword and asked the question, "Are you for us, or for our adversaries?" the answer should have been, "I am with you, Joshua" or "I am with your enemies." But the man said, "No." The implication was "Neither . . . I Am." This was God himself speaking to Joshua, which explains Joshua's response. Further instructions to Joshua from "the man" were to remove his sandals because the place on which he was now standing was holy. Without argument, Joshua obeyed and worshiped.

Like Joshua, when we are fighting giants and attempting to possess the land, we are called to worship the living God. Part of worshiping is trusting in God's direction for our lives. We are in the presence of a holy, faithful God, looking for His purposes.

What is God calling you to possess? Are you fighting to live the life God has called you to as a believer? Are there giants in the land? There always seem to be giants in our lives. King David, while still a mere boy, responded to the giant in his land: "Then David said to the Philistine, 'You come to me with a sword and with a spear and with a javelin, but I come to you in the name of the LORD of hosts, the God of the armies of Israel, whom you have defied'" (1 Sam. 17:45 ESV).

David made it clear as he responded to Goliath. All of the weapons David listed should be feared, but not by David, who had the right perspective. David said, "I come to you in the name of the LORD of hosts, the God of the armies of Israel, whom you have defied." While Saul's army cowered, shaking in their sandals, David got it. It's not the intimidating things before us that matter, but God, who promises to come with us as we possess the land.

David was outraged at Goliath's defiance, "this uncircumcised Philistine, that he should taunt the armies of the living God" (v. 26) and offered to do battle in the name of almighty God, his God. He told Saul, "Let no man's heart fail" (v. 32). David would kill their enemy. His older brothers mocked him and thought he was boasting, since he was just a shepherd boy and Goliath was an experienced warrior, and a big one at that.

Yet David was convinced that his God, who had rescued him many times before in the face of danger while he was tending sheep, would deliver him even now. As the account goes, God helped him choose humble, though familiar, weapons and honored his faith "that all the earth may know that there is a God in Israel" (v. 46).

That is the result of our faith when we're outnumbered by the Enemy. The world will know it was God. So where are your giants, and how do you expect to defeat them? We must go through our giants, not cower before them, in order to possess the land.

WHEN YOU SAY, "I CAN'T GO ON," LEAN INTO HIM, WAIT ON HIM (IN PRAYER)

Abba Father is living, faithful, and true. He will keep a covenant with you and bring you through.

We're not saying you can force yourself to be up to any challenge. None of this can be accomplished by somehow mustering up the strength and courage to go on. God has promised He will accomplish "a good work" in you and bring you home. What a reassuring ring that has.

This life is often hard and full of challenges. Therefore, when we get tired, we must find a way to take a break and wake the next morning refreshed, knowing that His mercies, along with hope and strength, are new every morning. He knows our limits; we can cast our full body weight on Him (1 Pet. 5:7).

When we need to relax and be affirmed, we can choose an activity we enjoy. There should be slowdowns in our intensity, and we need to rest between battles. Lamentations 3:22–25 gives a beautiful promise: "The steadfast love of the LORD never ceases; his mercies never come to an end; they are new every morning; great is your faithfulness. 'The LORD is my portion,' says my soul, 'therefore I will hope in him.' The LORD is good to those who wait for him, to the soul who seeks him" (ESV).

God has compassion on us and gives us mercies every day. They're available first thing. If you stop and think about it, we experience His mercies all the time; but when we're tired and weary of the battle, we lose sight of this fact. Jeremiah, the writer of Lamentations, said God is our "portion" (v. 24). He fills us up and becomes all that's needed for us to keep going through this life. However, there is a prerequisite: We must "wait for Him" (v. 25). When it looks as though nothing is happening, we are probably waiting. His movement in our lives doesn't necessarily happen when it's convenient for us. His timing often is not ours.

The Hebrew word for *wait* means "to look for, hope, expect." As we wait, we actively expect God to move into our situation. The other part of the Lamentations passage says to seek Him, and the definition for the Hebrew phrasing used here is "to seek deity in prayer and worship." We continue loving the Lord and worshiping Him because of all His awesome qualities. Life can be filled with expectation, and our hearts should look forward to how God will work during this time.

Still, we get overwhelmed by our situations, so God offers a word of direction and encouragement: "Take My yoke upon you and learn from Me, for I am gentle and humble in heart, and you will find rest for your souls. For My yoke is easy and My burden is light" (Matt. 11:29–30).

Do we handle life's challenges by being "yoked"? A yoke is a harness used on animals to plow the land. If the animals are not used to or new to the yoke, they would pull against each other. When this happened, no plowing would be accomplished. The animals had to be in sync and dependent on each other to move forward. Only when they relied on and trusted each other would results ensue. This is a lot like the way the Lord works with us when we allow ourselves to be yoked to Him. He teaches us and carries much of the load. We must trust His leading and rely on Him. What a powerful image to help us understand Jesus' teaching in Matthew 11.

Our yoke doesn't seem light or easy, does it? If we only look at the burden without getting into the harness, it is heavy and very hard. But when we are yoked with Jesus, we take on His load, one especially designed for us at this stage of our development, and we pull alongside Him, trusting His capability to find our direction. Compared to carrying our own burdens and trying to figure out our own paths, being in the harness with Jesus is simple. He bears the burden of making it easy to follow His lead and learn from Him.

INTIMACY AND PERSEVERANCE GO HAND IN HAND

What is intimacy with God? Is it going to church each week? Maybe making Christian friends? Intimacy must include the idea of knowing who God is and what He does for us. It's also letting ourselves be known, not trying to hide those parts of us that feel vulnerable. Knowing Him and being known by Him are both necessary, as they are in any other intimate relationship.

To persevere in life is to last long with God, and perseverance comes by being intimate with Him. One way to get to know the Savior, the Creator, the Comforter is by reading the Bible from beginning to end. Coming into His presence in earnest prayer is another way. When you're able to know God, you're able to last. Second Corinthians 4:5–7 makes this truth clear: "For what we proclaim is not ourselves, but Jesus Christ as Lord, with ourselves as your servants for Jesus' sake. For God, who said, 'Let light shine out of darkness,' has shone in our hearts to give the light of the knowledge of the glory of God in the face of Jesus Christ. But we have this treasure in jars of clay, to show that the surpassing power belongs to God and not to us" (ESV).

Here the apostle Paul described pure intimacy in various ways. The phrase "has shone in our hearts" means that God is in our hearts shining the light of Jesus Christ, so that we can know His glory and our relationship to Him. When we don't know Him, we dwell in darkness.

What is the "treasure in jars of clay"? It's when the Holy Spirit takes up residence in us. He shows that the power is not from us, but from God. It's all Him.

I (Beth) once watched a potter mold clay into a vase. He seemed to be completing his clay pot when he stopped, looked at it, crumbled the clay, and started over. He wanted the best pot, so he was going to remake that lump of clay. This pot was obviously intended to hold something. Like a pot, we are made to hold something as well: God's Spirit. Only by containing God in this way are we able to show His "surpassing power," one of the very attributes that make up His nature.

Like the potter, God keeps working on us until we are shaped to proclaim Him by our very lives. He continually molds us, working all the parts, and allows our experiences to achieve this end. He takes us through loss and suffering, blessing and abundance, to form the patterns of Jesus and stamp His image on the clay of our lives. This process is gradual. We used to live for ourselves, but now we live for Him. Old habits are stripped away. New gratitude and compassion take their place, until the treasure, which is God himself, is all that can be seen. It is He—not us—who does this wonderful work in our lives.

Finally, Jesus came to give freedom, which requires relearning and letting go of anything that becomes an idol. Idols are an abomination to God. They serve as substitutes for an authentic relationship with Him. In the Old Testament, God warned the children of Israel to keep the covenant He made with Moses and live in the land He had given them. When they were slaves in Egypt, that nation oppressed them. But God delivered them from Pharaoh and led them into Canaan. However, they first had to displace the people who lived there and destroy their system of idol worship. Yet the very ones God redeemed out of slavery preferred what those around them had, and exchanged their unique position with their God for worthless idols.

Even today, we find ways to do this. We can recognize this tendency when we ask, "What's not working? What's missing? Why?" Chances are, our own meager efforts or those of our culture have replaced our dependence on the Lord and His provision, such as grace, joy despite our circumstances, peace with Him, the freedom to live as He intended us to with unconditional love, and so on. As we choose to submit to His methods of transformation by faith, we relearn how to live with Him at the center. It's only His grace that accomplishes this, and the cross was the price of our freedom. This grace walk is a lot like walking on water, supernaturally accomplished.

We hope by now you're beginning to appreciate how our losses and suffering are tutors, training us in wisdom and discernment. We don't know of any other way to learn some of these lessons and become more like the Savior. But we must admit our inadequacies to be given His adequacy. The qualities Jesus exhibited while on earth are the same ones we need: having faith in the face of giants, listening to the Father and leaning into Him, practicing intimacy by knowing God and allowing Him to know us, prayerfully waiting and trusting in the waiting, dismissing idols, and walking in freedom.

It's a good thing we have so many models in the pages of Scripture, so we can glimpse what possessing the land means. Potters and earthen jars, yokes and burdens, battles and warriors all provide visual aids, like in Jesus' parables. Next, we'll see how John explained this process in an organic way. The Father won't give up on us until we get it. If we continue to walk with or be carried by Him, our faithful, holy God is committed to save us, time after time. And just as it was for the children of Israel, it's a zigzag journey for us today, full of grace.

10

We have learned much from gardeners in our area over the years, and our yard is the better for it. Along the way, we discovered these same principles can be applied to life and loss and actually reflect much of what Scripture teaches. John 15:1–16 explains this process of growth in adversity in these garden terms. The Vine is the source of life, and the Gardener tends the vineyard. The job of the branch, the believer, is to abide (remain, dwell) in the Vine.

COMPOST BRINGS HEALTHY GROWTH

Now that you've allowed us to help you dig into your stories, keep turning the dirt over. In regards to compost, living matter needs to be stirred so it doesn't become stagnant and putrid. The good bacteria breaks down bigger chunks of discarded materials into useable natural chemicals and minerals for the garden.

Spiritually speaking, prayer is a way to process those difficult areas that want to harden into unmanageable problems. A bit like the bacteria, though it's more than that. Prayer makes use of our connection to the life source we need. Prayer is both speaking and listening. It's what should happen in the garden of our hearts. It demonstrates that vital union with the Vine.

To plant a garden one must first till and break up hard soil. Then it's a good idea to amend with compost. That will create an ideal medium for life. After a long, hard winter, successful gardeners prepare their planting beds by softening the hard soil and possibly adding nutrients.

Similarly, Bible study plows the compacted attitudes (beliefs) and stubborn clay of our souls. God's Word introduces new ideas that will transform us. It feeds our souls and needs to remain in us. Regular Bible reading and application keeps the soil broken up and receptive to new seed. If this practice is followed, the master Gardener has a much easier time producing fruit. Prepared soil bears much fruit.

The spiritual compost comes from those trials and other instances that may seem purposeless at the time but ultimately have great value to the harvest. Someone who kept a thriving compost bin once explained this process of decay to us. He said the very center of the pile grows extremely hot because something wonderful is happening to convert that garbage into life-giving matter. Chemical reactions over time provide precious nutrients from things we didn't value or welcome. Change happens—over time—to manage the circumstances.

Little shoots can thrive now. However, tender shoots can be subject to devastating conditions: hail, bugs, diseases, blight, drought, and so on, stress these young plants. Yet in our gardens, as in our lives, as trials appear, their introduction can make for stronger yields. Adversity is unavoidable. Yet adversity is a medium for richness when it has matured. Therefore, we must yield in the trials and be teachable to grow faith.

Fairly soon after the plants are in, some new growth will be undesirable. Explore some of the suppositions surrounding loss and you'll probably find toxic ideas. These need to be uprooted like weeds. Toxic presuppositions (commonly held, unchallenged beliefs) are difficult to recognize, but if we aren't willing or able to explore them, they will become traps to keep us stuck and choke out our fruitfulness. Finding life in loss results from moving on to new levels of awareness and rescue. Here are some examples of risky assumptions or expectations:

- Families should come together in a crisis.
- In loss, people (and friends) should know what to do to help.
- If I work hard and long, I deserve to retire and live comfortably.
- If I raise my kids with love, they will live responsibly.
- If I take care of myself reasonably and live moderately, I won't get sick.
- If I persist in prayer, I will get the answer I am praying for.

Do you see the traps? We make assumptions on how life is supposed to be, and when it doesn't follow our predictions, we get thrown off track. "Meet my needs (disguised demands)" is the motto of toxic ideas.

Instead of working through brokenness, we just keep demanding our way. Jesus' teachings need to replace these faulty notions so that His "joy and delight may be in [us], and that [our] joy and gladness may be of full measure and complete and overflowing" (John 15:11 AMP).

When we challenge false assumptions, others may become disoriented and upset that we didn't leave these ideals alone. But that shouldn't deter us. If we change for the good while others expect us to be predictable, this change is also part of the pruning or cleansing.

BACK TO WEEDS—SOME EVALUATION IS NEEDED

Let's take a closer look at the weeds, the false assumptions and expectations in our lives, and answer a few key questions: How deep are the roots? How long have they been there? How hard is the soil? How motivated are you to get rid of them?

The longer these weeds go unrecognized and untended, the harder they are to remove and the more invasive they are for the garden. This leads to a critical spirit, which becomes resentment, then bitterness, and worse. Instead of facing the issue and taking action, we can deny there's a problem or cover it up or let others deal with it. We can even call it something else. Plus, our gardens looks about the same as others. What's wrong with that?

Consequently, the matter of motivation becomes the central issue. Motivation depends on several things, such as how much work a task will take (discomfort), over how much time (inconvenience), and what methods it will require to restore my garden (cost). So, we tend to neglect the weeds.

Here is a comparison between desirable new growth (things spiritually accomplished) and weeds (fleshly growth from our toxic presuppositions). These are not necessarily opposites, just related:

New Growth	Weeds
Peace	Comparison
Faith	Resentment
Kindness	Selfishness
Forgiveness	Gossip
Patience	Fear

As you can tell, this is not an exhaustive list. But there is a simple way to recognize the difference between the two: whatever is not of love or according to truth (Christlike) qualifies as a weed. Nevertheless, we can learn to like our weeds because they are familiar. They bloom year after year. But then they crowd out the healthy growth (richer, better fruit) and become invasive. That's when they are no longer tolerated. Ridding our gardens of weeds can be costly, uncomfortable, and inconvenient. But the alternative is living with weeds.

What methods do many novice gardeners employ? Easy ones — whack the heads off so you can't see them and let them blend into the yard. But there is a better way.

First, identify and name specifically what the weed (sin) is. Then get someone or something to help. This could be a friend, a sermon, a radio message, a printed resource, a portion of Scripture, or a prayer. There are any number of resources.

Second, apply the appropriate substance to eliminate the weed, not too toxic but still effective. This would be confession as you let the Holy Spirit reveal this issue and lead you in prayer. Start with what God is showing you. Also, input from a Christian counselor, a codependency workshop, or other timely seminar may help connect cause with effect and is good for recommending appropriate measures. Even Bible reading can accomplish this. What would be ineffective is just spreading "weed killer" on others rather than only looking at yourself. That's their property to tend, not yours. Ask, "What is my responsibility?" It's not to fix everybody else but to own your own stuff.

Third, repeat. Persist seasonally, regularly. Make a habit of it. Learning to rely on the master Gardener and permit His work in your life is a lifelong process, but a worthy one. Letting Him show you how to walk in His ways and love others is invaluable. If you don't persist, you default to selfish, self-serving attitudes and behaviors that defeat you and prolong your pain. The world teaches, "I'm not getting what I want . . . need . . . deserve." Thoughts like these will propagate and cause unnecessary hurt to others too. It's much better to be a friend of God and lay down your life. In this way, you can keep bearing fruit that remains. The fragrance is unmistakable.

When I (Beth) finished college in Arizona, Dave and I were ready for a change of climate and needed a fresh start. The Lord led us to live in beautiful Northern California, between the wine country of Sonoma County and the Pacific Ocean. Raised as Midwesterners, we wanted seasonal change but not drastic, oppressive weather. A delightful benefit to living in this region was we could experience visual reminders that change is good and necessary. Each season lasted for a time and then gave way to another purposeful season. All it took was a drive to view the hilly slopes of the wine country to appreciate how dormancy was important for new, fresh buds, then eventually full flower and fruit, and always harvest and vibrant color before the cycle started all over again. All God's handiwork, all planned for.

People in other places experience similar scenes from nature. Our season in Sonoma County lasted two years, just enough time to let God give blessings and some trials designed to help us grow closer to Him before He took us out of this rural paradise and into the Silicon Valley with its density and faster pace. All planned for— to learn new lessons, to submit to more pruning. Abide in the Vine; dwell there. He in us and we in Him, every season.

11

A LIFESTYLE OF RESTORATION

It's our conviction that after loss it is possible to walk in wholeness, regardless of the nature of that loss, but it will take living this new life. We can't remain as we were before. Union with Christ and His promised resurrected life is necessary to sustain us, despite the brokenness. It will take a rock and a refuge to keep us from giving into fear and despair.

Loss can disable, but it need not disqualify. Knowing the Savior, who keeps on saving us, and making choices to follow Him pave the way to beauty, richness, and abundance. Now it's time to review and then cement some life-giving truths into our conscious awareness.

Life is full of loss, and we need strategies to deal with it. When we are young, we're mostly concerned with acquiring and adding things to our lives, but the older we get, the more we need to allow loss as part of life and develop a recovery plan.

Common reactions to loss include anger or outrage. Someone might say, "That's not fair!" Another may cry out, "That's not supposed to happen now." Someone else, exhausted by self-effort, might say, "I can get through this." What follows is running, seeking expensive distractions, self-medicating, or attempting to replace what was lost with substitutes, counterfeits, or idols. Have you seen this happen? What are you tempted to do with your loss? Make a note to pray about this.

What must the antidote be for surviving loss? Is there a remedy for people going through the loss of a loved one, a job, a house, or so many other things? A. W. Tozer believed the remedy is what he called a "fixed center." He said, "Take God as He is and adjust accordingly. He never changes."[1] A fixed center is that by which everything else is measured.

What is your fixed center? Is your fixed center reflective of a self-focused society: "It's about *me*"? The Scriptures suggest a fixed center dependent on Christ. Paul told of his need for Christ to be his fixed center: "Indeed, we felt that we had received the sentence of death. But that was to make us rely not on ourselves, but on God who raises the dead" (2 Cor. 1:9 ESV). This position was a complete reversal for Paul, a former self-appointed antagonist of Christ-followers.

God uses events in our lives to teach us to lean on Him. You could use the term this verse of Scripture uses: *rely*. God allowed Paul to experience severe circumstances that forced him to rely not on what he could do but on what God could do through him. It all points to trusting God and not ourselves.

How does a fixed center look in a person's life? King Nebuchadnezzar in the Old Testament showed us both vantage points—the "It is I" perspective as well as the beauty of a man, even a powerful man, who looked to God (Dan. 4:22–33). Foolish Nebuchadnezzar believed that he was the great man who built Babylon, and it was all for him. "Look at the power I have. See my greatness," he essentially said. Have you ever been there? Do you get wrapped up with all you have done and miss the point? Many of us have done this, but the point is God is in control and gets the credit, not us.

This loss God warned Nebuchadnezzar about was fulfilled to drive him to another fixed center, one other than himself. "He was driven from among men and ate grass like an ox, and his body was wet with the dew of heaven till his hair grew as long as eagles' feathers, and his nails were like birds' claws" (v. 33 ESV).

What happened to the king? He became an animal and lost the kingdom he thought he built. Can you imagine the people of Babylon? Imagine the people talking: "Did you see the king today? He was out in the park eating grass and running around on all fours. And what's up with his hair?" What a "sentence of death." But that's not the whole story: "But at the end of that period I, Nebuchadnezzar, raised my eyes toward heaven and my reason returned to me, and I blessed the Most High and praised and honored Him who lives forever; for His dominion is an everlasting dominion, and His kingdom endures from generation to generation" (v. 34).

Could God be working in your life, through loss, to have you refocus and allow Him to become your fixed center? He is doing this in our lives, refining our fixed centers and continuing to perform this work in us.

Now we're ready to look at restoration as a lifestyle. These ideas are just a starting point to help you consider some new patterns and choices.

SURRENDER ALL AND LET HIM TEND TO THE WOUNDS

While vacationing on the East Coast, we hopped a ferry to Block Island for the day to ride our bikes. After an hour or so, we stopped at a beach at the end of a road. I (Dave) dismounted and instantly spotted an unusual rock. It was flat, black, and completely smooth, like a rock that had been in a tumbler for some time to eliminate all the rough edges. I picked it up and brought it home because it reminded me of a life that's changing, becoming smoother and more even after life buffets it. In Job 42, we're told how to surrender and allow this process to smooth out our own rough edges: "Then Job answered the LORD and said, 'I know that You can do all things, and that no purpose of Yours can be thwarted. . . . Therefore, I have declared that which I did not understand, things too wonderful for me, which I did not know. . . . I have heard of You by the hearing of the ear; but now my eye sees You; therefore I retract and repent in dust and ashes'" (vv. 1–3, 5–6).

We surrender by repenting in humility. We humbly come before God, our God, and confess any sins to Him and give Him back control of our lives. The other part of surrender is to allow God to attend your wounds. We all have wounds, and it is necessary to give them to the Lord, who is faithful in soothing and healing them.

PRACTICE HEAD-TO-HEART COMMUNICATION

When we talk about the "head," we mean knowing things about God—head knowledge. We may even know what God considers valuable and necessary. "Heart," though, refers to living out what we know. Knowing God changes our lives only when the truth of belonging to Him fills our thinking and reminds us of how valuable we are in God's sight. Then we can actually accept this fact in our hearts, not just in our heads. A helpful phrase is "belonging to and beholding Him."

When we get to know God on this level, we can trust Him for all that He is in our lives. Isaiah 26:4 states, "Trust in the LORD forever, for the LORD GOD is an everlasting rock" (ESV). It is true. We need to trust Him in all of life, especially when we deal with loss, because God is an everlasting rock. He is strong, powerful, and doesn't change with the wind. We can depend on Him no matter what.

We can trust God to be powerful, capable of handling any situation life throws at us. We put our confidence in Him for all things. "The steadfast of mind You will keep in perfect peace" (Isa. 26:3). Peace is the result of placing our trust in God.

VALUE SUPERNATURAL REALITIES

While we were writing about these attributes of a God-centered reality, I (Dave) had to confess that this one confused me. I really didn't get it until recently, and it took some wrestling.

To start with, we believe nothing gets past God. You will never hear God say, "Oh no! That slipped by Me. How did that happen?" God always has control, even in loss. He's in control of it all. Sometimes I have to admit that I wonder what's going on, but I just have to rest in His plan. Acceptance of this point is the goal. Notice what Isaiah 25:1 says: "O LORD, you are my God; I will exalt you, I will give thanks to Your name; for You have worked wonders, plans formed long ago, with perfect faithfulness."

God formed plans in eternity past for today and tomorrow. There is meaning in that. The rest of Isaiah 25 reveals the progression of God's salvation to His people. He is their "defense . . . refuge . . . shade from the heat." He will "prepare a lavish banquet . . . on this mountain." He will "swallow up death for all time. . . . It will be said in that day, 'Behold, this is the God for whom we have waited . . . let us rejoice in His salvation'" (vv. 4, 6, 8–9).

When we talk about loss and the pain of it all, it's those supernatural realities Isaiah reveals that we have to count on. Acceptance will gradually come as an act of grace. Only as we embrace those truths found throughout Scripture that speak of this puzzling aspect of life on earth can we walk in step and not resist. Life is lived in two dimensions: the literal passing of time and the ever-present eternal sphere. It's His perfect faithfulness that matters, and it's up to Him to make meaning from things we don't understand. As we value supernatural realities, we'll be supplied with meaning and acceptance.

REMEMBER, IT'S ALL ABOUT HIM

When life gets stripped down to the essentials, and we lose even some of those, we get confused. Jesus asked the Twelve, and anyone else who says they want to follow Him and go the distance, how do you feel about risking it all? Will you still follow Me and allow Me to be all I can be in your life? Will you let Me surround you, hold you up, and fill you with myself? (See John 6:66–69).

We recently taught a workshop to a group of bereaved parents. In addition to our workshop, other presenters taught principles of life after loss, though without God's involvement. They offered other options. The presentations ranged from a fairly broad and fuzzy acknowledgment of a higher power; to using a quote from the Bible (often poorly applied); to enlisting the help of mediums, dream therapy, poltergeists, animism, and the occult. We wondered why we were there. However, God reassured both of us and made it clear we were there to be His witnesses and ambassadors for the living God. It was all about Him. We were clearly outnumbered, but that's not a challenge for our omnipotent God.

How do you let God be involved in your life to this depth? You die. You give up your life and assume His life in you. Like Peter in the passage in John 6, we have realized through our losses that Jesus has the words of eternal life. There is no one, and nothing else, to match this. Peter was right: "Lord, to whom shall we go?" (v. 68).

We have also come to know, by faith and experience, that Jesus is the Holy One of God. Jesus gave His life for each one of us, knowing we would face these difficult days with Him in us, through us, around us, and with us. That's the message we left with that eclectic group of bereaved parents.

HOLD ALL THINGS LOOSELY

It doesn't take too long as we live in this world to realize things come and go. All things. Not long ago, while lying wide awake early in the morning, I (Beth) was looking at Dave as he slept. I was thinking, "I want to be with you every day." It was good he didn't wake up startled. Soon my eyes brimmed with tears as I stared right at him. The Lord had given me an unsettling thought: "It might not be this way tomorrow. He might be gone."

My dear Lord was reminding me to hold all things loosely, even people. God is the gift giver. He is the one who so generously gives, and also the one who may take away. It's His right to do so. Holding all things loosely is the way we need to live until we are face-to-face with our heavenly Father. All He entrusts us with or gives us to enjoy is ours only for a season. Our times are in His hand, as are our families, whom He gives us to love and take care of as good stewards. It's better for God to not have to pry away or unlock our fingers from the things or people He has loaned to us. They should not be clutched so tightly that He can't just gently take them.

I (Beth) remember from my childhood "borrowing" something that wasn't mine to keep and hearing my mom say, "Open your hand and let me have it." She was asking me to release my grip so she could take the object from me. This was uncomfortable at the time, and I really wanted to keep the thing that attracted me. We didn't struggle over it, as I recall, but I trusted she knew what was right.

That experience taught me that not all things are mine to keep just because I want them. Even people, homes, or jobs we all often lay claim to. These may have to be forfeited someday. When our perspective is such that we accept the things we love as temporary, it stings but doesn't have to destroy us when they go away. We loosely hold on to what's loaned to us because we are mere stewards, not possessors. It's all part of living this life now.

Someday, maybe very soon, God's Son will return to give us a lasting inheritance that nothing can take away. If we know Him, it's already reserved. In the meantime, we are waiting for that which is permanent and lasting to be revealed.

LET THINGS ON EARTH RECEDE

Sometimes, in the midst of our struggles, it helps to take a deep breath and focus on some comforting truths shared by Jesus, who fully understands our often unsettled hearts:

Therefore I tell you, do not be anxious about your life, what you will eat or what you will drink, nor about your body, what you will put on. Is not life more than food, and the body more than clothing? Look at the birds of the air: they neither sow nor reap nor gather into barns, and yet your heavenly Father feeds them. Are you not of more value than they? And which of you by being anxious can add a single hour to his span of life? And why are you anxious about clothing? Consider the lilies of the field, how they grow: they neither toil nor spin, yet I tell you, even Solomon in all his glory was not arrayed like one of these. But if God so clothes the grass of the field, which today is alive and tomorrow is thrown into the oven, will He not much more clothe you, O you of little faith? Therefore do not be anxious, saying, "What shall we eat?" or "What shall we drink?" or "What shall we wear?" For the Gentiles seek after all these things, and your heavenly Father knows that you need them all. But seek first the kingdom of God and his righteousness, and all these things will be added to you. Therefore, do not be anxious about tomorrow,

for tomorrow will be anxious for itself. Sufficient for the day
is its own trouble. (Matt. 6:25–34 ESV)

How many times do you see the word *anxious* in what you just
read? Why do you think it is repeated so often? Do we want to have
intimacy with God, or worry about things over which we have little control? So much of life is actually out of our control. It's an
illusion to think we keep our little world spinning. Look at the
examples Jesus used: birds, flowers, grass, and finally, our lifespan
itself. Our lifespan is really the issue for most of us. If we could just
control that!

Here Jesus presented a reality check. It's God who is in charge
of taking care of us; He doesn't just care for things in nature. Each
day has enough trouble of its own, so quit worrying about what
might or might not happen. We should instead concentrate on seeking "the kingdom of God and his righteousness" for our lives. It's
only when this is our first consideration that He promises to add all
these other things (v. 33).

Consequently, let's not confuse our part with God's. It's an exercise in futility. Our part is to seek Him; His part is to know what we
need. We will be blessed if we keep this straight. Do we really want
His righteousness more than the things of this world? Honestly think
about that. Jesus said, "Blessed are the pure in heart, for they shall
see God" (Matt. 5:8). Letting things on earth recede reflects a heart
that is pure. It's then we open ourselves to "seeing" Him.

Here's another truth that reveals where we place our values: "Do
not lay up for yourselves treasures on earth, where moth and rust
destroy and where thieves break in and steal, but lay up for yourselves
treasures in heaven, where neither moth nor rust destroys and where

thieves do not break in and steal. For where your treasure is, there your heart will be also" (Matt. 6:19–21 ESV).

The question implied here is this: What's important—things here on earth or things in heaven? The answer determines where we spend our energy and resources. Doing the work God has given us to do for the time that we're here, is laying up treasures in heaven. By the power and guidance of the Holy Spirit, we can each serve our families, the body of Christ, even strangers, from the heart. Then we leave the results with Him. It's such a great way to live.

TASTE HIS GOODNESS AND INTEGRATE FAITH IN THE SMALL THINGS

How often in the course of the day do we recognize the goodness of the Lord in events that we haven't planned? Things that test us. Those opportunities are just as important to building faith as things we gladly anticipate or routinely expect.

These verses from James give helpful guidance for remembering God's work in unplanned circumstances:

Count it all joy, my brothers, when you meet trials of various kinds, for you know that the testing of your faith produces steadfastness. And let steadfastness have its full effect, that you may be perfect and complete, lacking in nothing. If any of you lacks wisdom, let him ask God, who gives generously to all without reproach, and it will be given him. But let him ask in faith, with no doubting, for the one who doubts is like a wave of the sea that is driven and tossed by the wind. For

that person must not suppose that he will receive anything
from the Lord; he is a double-minded man, unstable in all
his ways. . . . Every good and perfect gift is from above,
coming down from the Father of lights with whom there is
no variation . . . due to change. (James 1:2–8, 17 ESV)

Walk through the day looking in the small places for God's presence and goodness. It's always there and we need to remember to
search for it. Yet such times produce only good in us. God plans
goodness, and we should make a habit of recognizing how this
occurs. It will build our faith and make us grateful, even when we
are still being tested. Again in James we read, "Blessed is a man
who perseveres under trial; for once he has been approved, he will
receive the crown of life which the Lord has promised to those who
love Him" (1:12).

Though this mind-set of supernatural realities and responses
seems challenging, it can become a lifestyle. Restoration is a process
of putting on and putting off. It starts with a fixed center on that
which cannot change. Everything else we experience is subject to
change. When we practice this, this understanding ushers in worship.
Recognizing all that we've been given, in spite of periodic times of
testing, transforms our response. We offer praise and thanksgiving,
honor and glory, not with our mouths alone but with our lives.

RECALLING WORSHIP

When you hear the word *worship*, what do you think of? In most
of my (Beth) early life, worship was an event—once a week. We

usually went to church to sing, pray, and hear a message, which stuck with me for a couple of days. That was worship. But Romans 12:1–2 talks about another kind of worship: "Present your bodies a living and holy sacrifice, acceptable to God, which is your spiritual service of worship. And do not be conformed to this world, but be transformed by the renewing of your mind, so that you may prove what the will of God is, that which is good and acceptable and perfect."

Worship is presenting our bodies, all that we are, as living and holy sacrifices. Ray Stedman was an author and pastor in California and noted as having said, "The problem with a living sacrifice is that it's always trying to crawl off the altar." Ever try to crawl off the altar? Worship is giving our lives to God and His plans. It's the reason we exist. When you have this understanding of worship, you sing a new song every day.

Recently I (Beth) was at a post office near our house, standing in line. As people do in a long line, I turned around to see who else was waiting with me. To my amazement, I noticed a person I hadn't seen in quite some time and wondered why she was even in our part of town.

After that long wait, and having taken care of my business, I greeted her. We visited for a few minutes. Planning to leave on other errands, I made a move toward the door when she asked, "Could you wait for me to finish? I'd like to continue our conversation."

I said, "Sure." As we talked some more, it became clear this meeting was planned for, an aspect of presenting my body as a sacrifice to God. Our conversation was difficult, and we had to clear up some issues. Yet I chose to wait and talk to her rather than be comfortable and leave. This meeting was a called-out event, arranged by a sovereign God. It was a form of worship to me.

BE STILL

Worship also includes learning to be still, letting Him quiet you. We worship by giving Him all our anxieties, fears, and doubts. As we confess these, we then agree with truth that He is God. Rest in His sovereignty, grace, and goodness.

A couple of nights ago, I (Beth) lay awake, unable to sleep. I was worrying about everything. First it was the finances and then an upcoming trip and all that needed to get done before we could leave. Then it was my grandson, then my car, then so many other things. It didn't seem to stop. I probably only slept two or three hours.

The weird thing is that we didn't have problems with finances. The trip planning was going well. My grandson was great and there was nothing wrong with my car. Why did this happen? I forgot my position as a child of the King until I remembered Isaiah 57:15: "For thus says the One who is high and lifted up, who inhabits eternity, whose name is Holy: 'I dwell in the high and holy place, and also with him who is of a contrite and lowly spirit, to revive the spirit of the lowly, and to revive the heart of the contrite'" (ESV).

My faithful God gave me peace when I gave Him my fears. I felt safe again, even at this season of life when so many things have hurt and confused me. But He is God, and I am not. He is sovereign, which means all that happens is *by His design*.

I normally don't care for formulas, but I'd like to share some things that have helped me. First, be patient and wait on Him. Second, let Him quiet all your thoughts and fears by releasing them to Him. Sometimes you have to release them to Him over and over again. Third, confess your sins, those things that separate you from God and His power. Fourth, consider truth. It's necessary to agree with the truths found in the Scriptures. Transformation happens when we seek and accept what God says in regard to the things we face. Fifth, rest in His design for your life and trust Him for your future. This process, this form of worship, is like CPR. It revives a troubled spirit. By it you have life again.

PRAISE HIS ATTRIBUTES, CHARACTER, AND GLORY IMPARTED

There are times in our lives when we must place ourselves facedown before our God. I (Dave) experienced this a few weeks after I learned about our son going home to be with our Lord.

I found myself home alone and restless. I tried turning on the TV, but there was nothing there for me. I got on my computer, yet didn't feel like answering e-mail. Then quite suddenly, I decided to turn up our sound system, very high, having put on worship music, and sing along with the musicians. Being so overwhelmed by God's presence, I just had to lie facedown in the living room praising Him for His attributes, character, and glory He shared with me. He is my salvation, and I have a deep need to praise Him.

USE YOUR GIFTS AND TALENTS FOR THE KINGDOM

You know, it takes commitment to the kingdom to value what God values, but there's freedom in that. When you live with loss, it's not that nothing else is important; but, more and more, as we place our hope in Him, we desire to use our gifts and talents to show

God's love to those we come in contact with as part of life. All believers have spiritual gifts, which are described in some key passages of Scripture (see 1 Cor. 12; Rom. 12; Eph. 4). These gifts require expression and are to be used to build up the body of Christ as the Holy Spirit leads. It's quite remarkable to think about. It's part of our calling to follow Him. We also commit our talents for God's use in building the kingdom. As we move through various times in our lives, we can perhaps appreciate new talents emerging, which should be investigated and developed.

How can your talents and gifts be given expression? What can you do for the kingdom that only you can?

LET MUSIC MINISTER WITH ITS MESSAGE AND BEAUTY

Not too long after we began experiencing our most recent losses, we started listening to music like we never had before. Whether Dave was driving to a friend's house some distance away, doing chores at home, or working on the computer, he listened to music with wonderful, life-giving messages. Beth also found that music needed to be a part of my routine. It became more intentional.

One of the songs we listened to over and over again was "Healer of My Heart." The lyrics ministered to both of us in precious ways. One day I (Dave) was out in the backyard doing a not-so-enjoyable task—weeding. I had my headphones in, listening to this song. Each time I heard the phrase "Healer of my heart," I'd pull a weed. I then would listen to the song again and pull more weeds. I did this for over two hours. What was happening? I was pulling physical weeds, but I was also pulling spiritual weeds of disbelief in God's love for me.

Two Scripture verses describe this process of healing through music: "I will incline my ear to a proverb; I will solve my riddle to the music of the lyre," found in Psalm 49:4 (ESV), and Psalm 101:1, which reads, "I will sing of steadfast love and justice; to you, O LORD, I will make music" (ESV).

Let music wash over your broken heart. Let it bring healing and release, and give words to the longing you feel. God speaks to us through music on a level that transcends mere thought.

FIND ROLE MODELS IN BOTH THE OLD AND NEW TESTAMENTS

Occasionally in the Scriptures we'll see God, through His chosen instrument at the time, call for a review. It reminded the people that they, in fact, were part of God's plan and could trust Him in their immediate circumstance as they had in times past. We also are encouraged to keep living in faith when we read of these places in the Bible.

Hebrews 11 puts this in perspective. It's the roll call of those who put faith on display, often in demanding circumstances. It says we can be sure of what we put our faith in and hope for. When I (Beth) need encouragement to keep going, I meditate on passages like this.

These people closed the jaws of lions, put out raging fires, and escaped from the swords of their enemies. Although they were weak, they were given the strength and power to chase foreign armies away. Some women received their loved ones back from death. Many of them were tortured, but they refused to be released. They were sure they would get a better reward when the dead were raised to life. They were poor, mistreated, and tortured. The world did not deserve these good people, who had to wander in deserts and on mountains and had to live in caves and holes in the ground. All of them pleased God because of their faith (see vv. 33–39).

It's a good practice to find our role models in the Word of God. Whom do you admire and want to be like because they followed God against the odds? Paul is mine because I can see his human failings, while his transformation of faith is also very apparent. God may put others in our lives today who move us to follow Jesus. Who are your role models? And as inconceivable as it might seem right now, you may be someone else's role model. Our walk of faith should inspire others to choose to keep at it.

Worship is a 24/7 affair. For the believer, it's as natural as breathing. It's our way of expressing our relationship with a holy and gracious God. It says, "I have a Redeemer who deserves my devotion." It also says, "I will believe in His Word that speaks life to me." It shows how we are connected to all those who have gone before us and have used their special gifts and talents to build the kingdom. Worship is as individual as our fingerprints, and should be done authentically.

NOTE

1. A. W. Tozer, *The Pursuit of God* (Las Vegas: IAP, 2009), 65–68.

12
AUTHENTICITY

Openness and sincerity, as opposed to imitation and phoniness, define authenticity. It's an aspect of character that's only truly available when one accepts Jesus' gift of new life. In secure dependence, masks can be stripped away. The need to cover up for fear of being genuine, no longer remains an issue. We are acceptable in the Beloved.

PRAY UNCEASINGLY, LETTING GOD CONTROL AND SUSTAIN

In Luke 11:2–4, we read Jesus' own instructions about prayer: "When you pray, say: 'Father, hallowed be your name. Your kingdom come. Give us each day our daily bread, and forgive us our sins, for we ourselves forgive everyone who is indebted to us. And lead us not into temptation'" (ESV).

It's been my (Beth) habit for some time now to write in a prayer journal once a week. When our family was young, I only shared my entries with Dave to make him aware of what was on my heart to pray about. But sometime when the boys were teenagers, we intentionally gathered together after dinner, a good time to reach them, and take turns talking about events, our needs, and anything else we knew the others could weigh in on or support with prayer.

All the while, my spiritual notebook was open so I could record what was said into two columns: praises and prayer. It was important to start by acknowledging our current blessings, and then other things would emerge. What a privilege to be part of this scene, especially when time demands were tight. I'd ask some questions: What do we need to confess to God as a family, as well as individually, and ask forgiveness for? What do you want to thank God for? What do we need to ask God for as a family, and as individuals?

One particular time remains especially vivid. We were having family prayer time with our two nearly grown sons, and Ian, the older one, revealed he was not going back to West Point. He was on Christmas break during his first year at the United States Military Academy. He also talked briefly about his plan B. I wrote the request for prayer in our family journal. We did not advise him, but we all went to prayer for Ian and for other needs. We remembered to praise God for His faithfulness to us.

The next morning, not knowing what I (Dave) would find, I got up early because it was the day Ian was supposed to return to West Point. I found my son, serious and deliberate, sitting in the living room all packed and ready to go. He had actually cleaned his bedroom and was wanting to grab breakfast burritos and a local newspaper before he got on the plane. God answers prayer. He would have answered our prayers if Ian went back to school or if he didn't return there. God had plans for Ian, and it was not up to us, as a family, to dictate our wants or needs to him and actually to God. This decision was between Ian and the Lord.

EXERCISE CHOICES AND ACCEPT
GOD'S WAY OF ESCAPE IN TEMPTATION

Life is about choices, every day of our existence. As we read the Scriptures, we find that choices need to be made by any of us to live righteous lives by the power God provides. We can choose to love the unlovely, bless those who persecute us, persevere in trials, ask God for wisdom when we're in short supply, have our minds renewed by immersing ourselves in His Word, and so on. These are practical choices based on personal needs.

We also find a need to guard against Satan and his plans against us. The answer to these attacks from our Enemy comes in the form of a promise found in 1 Corinthians 10:13: "No temptation has overtaken you that is not common to man. God is faithful, and he will not let you be tempted beyond your ability, but with the temptation he will also provide the way of escape, that you may be able to endure it" (ESV).

What is being said here is there is nothing new under the sun. All people have experienced these temptations. In addition, God gives us a way out, but we are required to look for it. Often, we can find our way of escape when the Holy Spirit whispers something He's already taught us from God's Word.

NO VEILS

The Lord is all about removing falseness or veils in our lives. Who are we trying to impress? Or fool? No hiding, self-righteousness, self-confidence, or self-pity.

Do you know what falls away when you live with loss? Your need to impress. By the power of the Holy Spirit, we can shed our false selves. It's refreshing to meet people who actually are what they appear to be. To be genuine is also refreshing. There's no wasted energy trying to hide our true selves. The apostle Paul told about Moses, who fell into this trap of hiding what was really there:

> Therefore having such a hope, we use boldness in our speech, and are not like Moses, who used to put a veil over his face that the sons of Israel might not look intently at the end of what was fading away. But their minds were hardened; for until this very day at the reading of the old covenant the same veil remains unlifted, because it is removed in Christ. But to this day whenever Moses is read, a veil lies over their heart; but whenever a person turns to the Lord, the veil is taken away. Now the Lord is the Spirit, and where the Spirit of the Lord is, there is liberty. But we all, with unveiled face, beholding as in a mirror the glory of the Lord, are being trans-formed into the same image from glory to glory just as from the Lord, the Spirit. (2 Cor. 3:12–18)

Paul was recounting how Moses had a problem with trying to impress others. When he had been with the Lord on Mount Sinai, his face literally glowed. When he returned to the camp, many could not look at his face because it was so bright. So Moses came up with a plan. He put a veil on his face and wore it every day. This was an instance when Moses was dealing with a temptation.

One day as he was getting ready to go out and be with the children of Israel, Moses noticed the glow on his face had lessened. What did he do? He put the veil on his face to hide what was no longer glowing. And what was the problem with this? He was covering up, not wanting the children of Israel to observe him after the glory faded.

Don't we do this? Have we put confidence in what God has accomplished through us, wanting to bask in that "glow." Aren't there times when we just want the attention? Who are we trying to impress?

We must tell ourselves, "Stop it already!" We *are* weak, but He is so strong. He makes up for all that we lack. We can allow God to be all we need at the moment, and He will allow our lives to represent Him.

KNOW YOUR LIMITATIONS

Know your limitations, because the Enemy does and will take advantage of them. God will point out these limitations. I (Dave) had a friend once say to me, "If God doesn't point out these limitations, your wife surely will!" There is some real truth to this statement. God can encourage people in our lives to clarify our limitations. So listen. Paul said there's a purpose in knowing and acknowledging our limits. "Indeed, we felt that we had received the sentence of death. But that was to make us rely not on ourselves but on God who raises the dead" (2 Cor. 1:9 ESV).

Limitations drive us to depend on God's power to live effective lives. I have discipled men for years and learned we all have limitations, but we can still be effective when we depend on God for power. My last discipleship group included someone who understood this in a significant way. He was a capable young man and a new Christian eager to grasp what God had for him. He finally realized he didn't have much to offer God and that became the most important breakthrough in his life so far. While many of us in the group had an unrealistic belief that we could handle much of what was thrown our way, this young man came to accept that he could only live life realizing it was only God, and not himself, who had real power.

REAL BELIEVING

The way to approach life when dealing with loss is with real belief at every turn, choosing faith in our difficulties, and keeping our eyes focused outward, not inward. We can't just look at ourselves and the troubling circumstances. Doing so paralyzes us. When we say choose faith in difficult circumstances, we mean it. If we don't live in faith, we won't make it through. Pretending will run out; we can cover up for only so long.

When life hurts and we don't feel ready to be used by God to help ease another's pain or bring encouragement, just the fact that we still believe is enough. God's messengers, the prophets, were acquainted with life in the pit. Jeremiah, Isaiah, Ezra, and so many others learned the discipline of believing, despite the evidence, that God was still working and would use them as part of the process.

Fear comes from thinking we have to solve our own dilemmas. Belief derives from being convinced that God is near, offering help.

Isaiah 41:10, 13 says, "Fear not, for I am with you; be not dismayed, for I am your God; I will strengthen you, I will help you, I will uphold you with my righteous right hand. . . . For I, the LORD your God, hold your right hand; it is I who say to you, 'Fear not, I am the one who helps you'" (ESV). These verses say it all. We are helpless apart from God and His mercy. This life is frightening at every turn, but then there's awesome, almighty God, who holds our hands. Our eyes of faith make it possible to accept this present reality. As we do, He'll use that faith and put it on display, showing the way to someone else who needs Him.

FORGIVE

Forgive like Stephen, who, while being stoned, offered intercession for the perpetrators:

Now when they heard these things they were enraged, and they ground their teeth at him. But he, full of the Holy Spirit, gazed into heaven and saw the glory of God, and Jesus standing at the right hand of God. And he said, "Behold, I see the heavens opened, and the Son of Man standing at the right hand of God." But they cried out with a loud voice and stopped their ears and rushed together at him. Then they cast him out of the city and stoned him. And the witnesses laid down their garments at the feet of a young man named Saul. And as they were stoning Stephen, he called out, "Lord Jesus, receive my spirit." And falling to his knees he cried out with a loud voice, "Lord, do not hold this sin against them." And when he had said this, he fell asleep. (Acts 7:54–60 ESV)

Who is throwing stones in your life? This could be friends or even family members who are attacking you because of the way you live. When we're attacked, we need to see eternal realities, just like Stephen saw in his stoning. He realized he was going to Jesus and said, like his Lord on the cross, "Lord, do not hold this sin against them" (v. 60). Instead of demanding his right to get even, he gave up his rights to the Lord.

That's the key: giving up our rights to Jesus. He will take care of it all, and He'll make it all right someday. "Never take your own revenge, beloved, but leave room for the wrath of God. . . . 'Vengeance is Mine, I will repay,' says the Lord. . . . Do not be overcome by evil, but overcome evil with good" (Rom. 12:19, 21).

HEARING HIS VOICE AND WAITING ON HIM

Sometimes in the Bible we read accounts in which God's voice thundered from the heavens, or when He made His will known by speaking directly to a prophet or someone like Moses or Abraham. Today, His Word does that for us. When we read it with the help of our teacher, the Holy Spirit, we hear His voice speaking to our minds and hearts. Anytime He does that for us, we need to determine His meaning and what our response should be. Is it to reveal truth we have never thought of, or to show us we are going in the wrong direction and need to turn around? Is it to reassure us that we, in fact, are doing the right things and need to continue to be faithful? Or could it be He is asking us to wait? Will we respond in kind?

Habakkuk, a prophet of God, lived in turbulent times, not unlike today. He was distressed and asked God, "How long, O LORD, will I call for help, and You will not hear?" (Hab. 1:2) When we are waiting, it may seem God is just hard of hearing or busy with someone else's problems. But that isn't the case. God answered Habakkuk, "Look among the nations! Observe! Be astonished! Wonder! Because I am doing something in your days—you would not believe if you were told" (v. 5).

In this small book we see with remarkable clarity God telling His prophet His plans to judge His people by using their enemies, but first Habakkuk had to wait on God's timing. God was judging His people for their idolatry, but Habakkuk saw only the wickedness of their enemy. To the prophet, life seemed out of control. He never imagined that God would use a people more wicked than they to accomplish His will. It wasn't the answer he expected or wanted to hear.

Are we like Habakkuk? Do we want answers now for the mess that surrounds us? When God is silent, do we assume He doesn't see or care? When we see evidence that things are getting worse and more complicated, do we accuse Him of not being capable of dealing with it? Habakkuk, like many today, didn't expect God to use some of the methods He does to accomplish His ends. We wouldn't do it that way.

In Habakkuk 3, the prophet accepted God's plan. It would definitely get worse before it got better. The enemy would come and carry out God's wrath, but then would come the deliverance and God's dealing with that enemy. Habakkuk responded with emotion and conviction: "I heard and my inward parts trembled. . . . Because I must wait quietly for the day of distress. . . . Though the fig tree should not blossom and there be no fruit on the vines, though the yield of the olive should fail and the fields produce no food . . . yet I will exult in the LORD" (vv. 16–18).

Can we do the same? When we see world events unfolding, bringing economic disasters, wars, or natural catastrophes all within a short period of time, will we still wait and listen for His voice? When there seems to be no relief in sight, will we still trust and even exalt His name? What other choice makes sense? If we understand God's character and the plans He has for His children, we can.

Micah, another of God's prophets, had a similar response when he said, "But as for me, I will watch expectantly for the LORD; I will wait for the God of my salvation. My God will hear me. Do not rejoice over me, O my enemy. Though I fall I will rise; though I dwell in darkness, the LORD is a light for me" (Mic. 7:7–8).

Micah also lived expecting imminent judgment from God. God had warned His people repeatedly, but no one took Him seriously. Micah, however, placed his hope in the God of his salvation. Micah's message was certain: The Lord will vindicate His people. He will listen and show the way, though times are dark and the enemy has the upper hand. Micah, like other Old Testament prophets, even prophesied the Messiah's birth in Bethlehem. Grace will triumph. God is a forgiving God, a redeeming God, and a faithful God.

As Jesus said, "But the Helper, the Holy Spirit, whom the Father will send in my name, he will teach you all things and bring to your remembrance all that I have said to you. Peace I leave with you; my peace I give to you. Not as the world gives do I give to you. Let not your hearts be troubled, neither let them be afraid" (John 14:26–27 ESV).

Listen for God in all your circumstances. He does speak to us, and it's always timely.

Years ago, I (Dave) served on staff at a large church as an administrator. One particular time when we waited for God's voice, we were having problems with people parking in the neighborhood in all the wrong places. The elders needed to make a decision before the next Sunday on how they would handle the parking issue or the city of Palo Alto would close down the church. The elders needed to be unanimous in their decision, but they didn't seem to be able to make a decision they all could agree on.

On Saturday night, they still had not made a decision when a call came from a church close by. They said they'd allow us to use their parking lot, since they were Seventh Day Adventists and didn't meet on Sunday. The elders chose to wait and listen for the Lord rather than do what they were being pressured to do. They heard His voice because they waited.

Authenticity is a character quality of God himself. He is trustworthy because there is no false way in Him. When we put our trust in Him instead of pulling our own strings, we reflect His nature. This response shows a faith that is maturing, living deep rather than staying on the surface with clichés and platitudes. It's piling up personal evidence in a God whose motives come from love and who's capable of growing us in meaningful ways.

13

LIVING DEEP

When you decide to turn to the Lord in your loss, you open the door to a new level of living above your circumstances. The living God keeps covenant with His children and will honor your intentions to go the distance with Him. Expect power and authority, purpose and resources in this arena. Existence, for those on this path, is a redeemed life, not mere survival. Follow God, childlike and meek. Make God the treasure, personal and exalted.

Many people believe following God means some formal ministry that you should do for God. Following God is powerfully described in Isaiah 61:1–3:

> The Spirit of the Lord GOD is upon me, because the LORD has anointed me to bring good news to the afflicted. He has sent me to bind up the brokenhearted, to proclaim liberty to captives and freedom to prisoners; to proclaim the favorable year of the LORD and the day of vengeance of our God; to comfort all

who mourn, to grant those who mourn in Zion, giving them
a garland instead of ashes, the oil of gladness instead of
mourning, the mantle of praise instead of a spirit of fainting.
So they will be called oaks of righteousness, the planting of
the LORD, that He may be glorified.

Isaiah described what it meant to follow God. The Spirit of God
will cause us to bring life to those around us, bringing good news,
binding up broken hearts, proclaiming liberty, and freeing people who
are in bondage. God will raise up those who are devastated by loss.
When he brings us such opportunities, we respond and follow His lead.

At the time Isaiah prophesied, the nation of Israel were being
held in captivity by their enemies. But he, nonetheless, was being
called into ministry by the power and provision of almighty God.
In our situation today, because of the Spirit bringing hope and healing to us, God will use us wherever we find people devastated in
life and looking for answers to difficult questions.

Your life can answer their questions. God is with you, granting
"the oil of gladness" and the "mantle of praise." We are also in the
process of becoming "oaks of righteousness, the planting of the
LORD, that He may be glorified." No shame. Desolation is not permanent to the offspring of the Lord.

We believe in divine appointments. We often have what appears
to be chance meetings with people but instead discover the joy of
representing Jesus on this earth. God arranges meetings with those
who need to hear or see something of Him. We have also been led
in the same way to be recipients of others' living out their faith.
They minister to us too. It's all part of the plan. The Lord's life lived
out is obvious and so needed.

EXPECT PURPOSE AND ASK, "HOW DO I RESPOND?"

We need to give away our lives each day. Our lives are not ours to keep if we gave them to Jesus. In Jeremiah 1:5, we see that God has a purpose for each life: "Before I formed you in the womb I knew you, and before you were born I consecrated you; I have appointed you a prophet to the nations."

Let's make this personal. The Lord comes to you in His Word and says something like, "Before you were born, I made you for a special purpose that only you have. Also, because I redeemed your life, you are holy and an object of My love. I will give you a cluster of spiritual gifts unique to you." We are made the way we are by our loving God. He knows us intimately and has created us to do good works.

God knows us in a special way. He knows us because He designed us for a purpose. It's part of His plan, which He is working out until we go to be with Him. By faith, we can learn what that is and cooperate with Him.

CULTIVATE INTIMACY WITH GOD, WHO KEEPS HIS COVENANT

Proverbs 3:5–8 may be a familiar truth, but let its words seep in slowly. Chew on each phrase. What is God showing you this time? For me (Beth), when the secondary losses were piling up and Dave was feeling life would never be fair again, the word *acknowledge* became my lifeline. "Trust in the LORD with all your heart and do not lean on your own understanding. In all your ways acknowledge Him, and He will make your paths straight. Do not be wise in your own eyes; fear the LORD and turn away from evil. It will be healing to your body and refreshment to your bones."

Each day I could acknowledge Him. Moment by moment, He would show me how and where; I was becoming aware of the "all" when I awoke to the brilliant Colorado sunshine in the middle of winter, took time to wander about my garden and smell the pungent fragrances of the native plants in the meadow, was with a friend, attended a concert in the park, or through any number of other everyday occurrences. To acknowledge is to let Him make my path straight, to take the roller coaster dips and smooth them out. If I acknowledged Him, I was not tempted to be wise in my own eyes. Revering my Lord kept me from evil. I wasn't just complaining, blaming, and looking for escapes. I acknowledged Him and didn't expect to "lean on my own understanding." All this builds intimacy.

We all want intimacy, don't we? Intimacy is thought of as a close, familiar, and affectionate or loving personal relationship with another person. We all need, and actually have been created to have, intimacy with the living God. It is almost as if there is a missing puzzle piece and God comes in and finishes the puzzle.

We are the object of His loyal love as well. Because He loved us, He grafted us into the Vine, the source of life and fruitfulness. Refreshment and healing are possible. We were created for renewal.

LIVE DEEP, NOT SHALLOW

Loss, in fact, has a positive side. It develops us in important ways. It pulls us out of the wading pool and into the deep end. We aren't left to flounder, thrash around in a panic, and go under, however. We have a blueprint for suffering that shows us the steps to take and the purposes accomplished at each level: "Therefore, since we have been justified by faith, we have peace with God through our Lord Jesus Christ. . . . Not only that, but we rejoice in our sufferings, knowing that suffering produces endurance, and endurance produces character, and character produces hope, and hope does not put us to shame, because God's love has been poured into our hearts through the Holy Spirit who has been given to us" (Rom. 5:1, 3–5 ESV).

Living deep comes at a price: surrender. But abundance awaits on the other side. We are "amply supplied," as Paul discovered when he was in a Roman prison. He learned the secret of contentment and living deep when his future was in doubt. Philippians is full of earnest entreaties backed up by tested experience. Christ was Paul's example and his source of strength in unthinkable circumstances.

The apostle said, "Rejoice in the Lord always; again I will say, rejoice! . . . The Lord is near. Be anxious for nothing, but in everything by prayer and supplication with thanksgiving let your requests be made known to God. . . . The things you have learned and received and heard and seen in me, practice these things, and the God of peace will be with you" (Phil. 4:4–6, 9).

We, as well as Paul, can do all things through Christ who strengthens us as we move from the shallow end to the deep end, being loved in order to love others in His name.

Another aspect of living deep is seeing others and their needs. Living in Christ brings freedom, often from ourselves. As our attitudes and actions align with His, we are freed from our selfish selves, which demand satisfaction: "For you were called to freedom, brethren; only do not turn your freedom into an opportunity for the flesh, but through love serve one another. For the whole Law is fulfilled in one statement: 'You shall love your neighbor as your-self.' But the fruit of the Spirit is love, joy, peace, patience, kindness, goodness, faithfulness, gentleness, self-control; against such things there is no law" (Gal. 5:13–14, 22–23).

Christ fulfilled the law and gave us two commands we can obey: Love the Lord and love others. It's interesting that we are to love oth-ers as ourselves. The Lord understands us to such a degree that He uses an example that makes sense to us. We take care of ourselves. We eat at least three times a day, shower and put on clean clothes that fit our intentions for the day, and so on. These activities imply one thing: We love ourselves. Consequently, God uses something we can appreciate and only our redeemed self is capable of. He says we should even "prefer" others before ourselves. Only in Christ can we forebear, show patience, and practice humility. His resources are ever available for this purpose. It's His covenant with us.

POWER AND AUTHORITY EXIST IN JESUS' NAME, NO MATTER THE TRIAL

Often when we suffer, we think we should be sidelined. Why? Are we no longer qualified to bring the good news of the gospel to others? In my (Beth) own case, because I knew in the deepest part of me that God keeps His promises to me in my suffering, I couldn't be silent. I wanted anyone who needed to know my God to meet Him and put their trust in Him to walk with them, too.

I had new authority and chose to use His power in the very midst of my heartbreak. Jesus' High Priestly Prayer of John 17 was being answered in the crucible of our lives. He was being glorified in me, and the Father was keeping me in His name and uniting me as one with my Lord (vv. 10–11). And don't ask me how, but His joy was being "made full" in me (v. 13).

The most amazing part is that we can experience hatred from the world because we are no longer like the world but still rise above it. Jesus specifically asked that we *not* be removed from this world but that we be kept "from the evil one" (v. 15). Instead, we are sent into the world just like Jesus was (v. 18). And He helps us endure in His name.

Jesus asked the Father to "sanctify" us in truth and His Word is that truth (v. 17). The Lord told His disciples the plan and didn't lead them on. He said, "These things I have spoken to you, so that in Me [not in our circumstances] you may have peace. In the world you have tribulation, but take courage; I have overcome the world" (John 16:33).

Because we are united with Jesus in the Godhead—Father, Son, and Holy Spirit, we can be "just as" they are (see John 17:21). Let that sink in a minute. The same power and authority for the same purpose, "that the world may know" (v. 23).

Finally, Jesus told the Father He had made known God's name (and all that it implies about His character and person) to mere men and women, boys and girls, "so that the love with which You loved Me may be in them, and I in them" (v. 26).

That's how it was designed. Jesus came, taught, healed, loved, and sacrificed to give us new life in Him. Now we live with the promises that He will redeem us and *is* redeeming us even now as we journey through this life. Our suffering is like His: It is only for a time, serves a greater purpose, and will result in joy. *Sanctification* involves growing in holiness. We grow more like our Lord by submitting to Him, just as Jesus did to the Father. We have all we need to fulfill our call as "sent" ones. But have we remembered to ask? Jesus told us to: "So also you have sorrow now, but I will see you again, and your hearts will rejoice, and no one will take your joy from you. In that day you will ask nothing of me. Truly, truly, I say to you, whatever you ask of the Father in my name, he will give it to you. Until now you have asked nothing in my name. Ask, and you will receive, that your joy may be full" (John 16:22–24 ESV).

We represent the living God and have power in Jesus' name. Someone once said this power is much like that of an automobile. Do we get into our cars and push them down the street? No, we get into our cars, turn the key which engages the engine, put the car into gear, and off we go. So why is it so hard to engage the power of God? He is already working. We just need to ask Him where He is sending and leading us and walk there with Him in the power that He supplies. He won't force His power on us. He waits until we ask. And, by the way, it would be best if He's in the driver's seat.

WANTING EACH DAY TO COUNT

Paul cautioned us in Ephesians, "Look carefully then how you walk, not as unwise but as wise, making the best use of the time, because the days are evil. Therefore do not be foolish, but understand what the will of the Lord is" (Eph. 5:15–17 ESV).

Making the best use of time has become such a burden in our lives. We don't want to miss an opportunity to make time count. For example, you can be on vacation and an opportunity will show up in your day, and you'll ask God if He wants you to respond or not and how.

Recently, we were attending other workshops as part of a grief conference where we were presenting. One particular workshop, I (Dave) made time to visit a seminar that was heavily attended and was advocating demonic activities. Within a minute or two, I began asking God what He wanted me to do or say.

What I heard in answer to my prayer was, "Not now." I began arguing with God and saying to Him, "I can handle this discussion. I know what to say." Whereupon I heard in my spirit again, "Not now; there are some things you don't know about that might create problems." So I listened to that and left the room.

That day I didn't get in the way of God's plan. There might be other days God says, "Go for it." Then I will be free to speak His truth wherever I find myself with no hesitation. Our days should count.

WARRIORS ALL

Like Daniel, Paul, Joseph, Ruth, Mary, Esther, and so many others who were called to live in submission, accepting unconventional methods of warfare, we are targets of the Enemy. But we, too, can be a living testimony to God's promised all-sufficiency.

There is no denying that life is a battle. But we are not unequipped or called to enter into the battle alone. We have seen in the pages of Scripture how God does battle around, for, and with us and extends His grace to those who'll receive it. We don't have the whole picture yet, but we know who does. We are the army of the Lord of hosts being led into skirmishes, small and great, on a regular basis and will have our reward in due time.

In the meantime, be assured, "The LORD your God is in your midst, a mighty [victorious warrior] who will save; he will rejoice over you with gladness; he will quiet you by his love; he will exalt over you with loud singing" (Zeph. 3:17 ESV).

By living deep, we have an eternal sense of why we're here doing battle: We're being given promised peace and joy, patience and mercy, wisdom and strength, blessing and abundance by the one "who stretches out the heavens, lays the foundation of the earth, and forms the spirit of man within him" (Zech. 12:1).

14

SACRED WISDOM

Some of the work of grief is learning what *not* to do. Two unhealthy, unproductive responses are to run and to blame. Though tempting, neither response will bring lasting satisfaction. The thing to do when overwhelmed by trials and heartache is submit. Go to the foot of the cross and look at Jesus' pure act of grace and let Him have all of you. Quit wrestling. Start the dialogue that will lead you through. Let Him quiet your spirit, soothe your mind, and create calm amidst the storm. You can't outrun the pain and longing; you can only offer it to Him in worship. Blaming a person, place, or thing won't change the outcome. It will only delay the work God can do in your own life.

PERSONAL REFLECTION

Excavate: deepening our roots. Read Genesis 3:8–13; 1 Kings 19:1–8; and John 11:21–32.

Extend: branching out. Notice how Adam and Eve were both guilty of running and blaming. Did this accomplish anything? How was Mary's response different from Martha's? Is it good to run even when we're afraid? How does God demonstrate that He cares about our troubles? With whom do you identify in these verses? Why?

Emerge: looking ahead. What is God saying to you? What will you do? As you look for this, how did you see this in action in your heart or life? (Provide an example and the date.)

The Enemy wants us to lose focus and drag around the death of depression instead of seeking hope from Jesus' own hand. Jesus' victory is for all time—in good times and bad. He is the finisher of our faith, which means we can't do it ourselves. As believers in Jesus Christ, we are called to submit to our Lord and His direction in our lives. Yet we sometimes fight submission. We question if we can handle things on our own or make the situation and our feelings go away. But we can't, no matter how much we want to.

However, God steps in to help us only as we allow Him to have access to all our thoughts and feelings. Giving Him all our pain is an act of worship. We lay it all at His feet. We were never meant to handle loss ourselves. Hebrews 12:1–3 gives perspective on this:

> Therefore, since we have so great a cloud of witnesses surrounding us, let us also lay aside every encumbrance and the sin which so easily entangles us, and let us run with endurance the race that is set before us, fixing our eyes on Jesus, the author and perfecter of faith, who for the joy set before Him endured the cross, despising the shame, and has sat down at the right hand of the throne of God. For consider Him who

has endured such hostility by sinners against Himself, so that you will not grow weary and lose heart.

WITNESSES WHO ENCOURAGE US

Those "witnesses surrounding us" (v. 1). are in both the Old and New Testaments. Think of those believers who loved God and faithfully followed Him. We also think of men and women who have touched our lives today. They're sent from the Lord.

I (Dave) has had a few mentors who've had a profound impact on my life. Ray Stedman, a gifted and humble pastor of an authentic New Testament church where I was called to serve, was one. Ron Ritchie, a friend and staff member of that same church, who discipled me into ministry was another. He showed me how to be faithful and love my Lord, shun legalism, and embrace grace. Earl Webb, a flying buddy, shares the love of Jesus with me in a quiet way. Hopefully, we all have these kinds of folks around us.

LAY ASIDE SIN

We are also reminded in this passage in Hebrews to "lay aside every encumbrance" (v. 1), and sin. Some are anger, fear, unforgiveness, sexual immorality, lying, pride, and many more. We are called to put them all aside. Let the Holy Spirit show you what these are and when they appear. Things like this that we don't renounce will continually trip us up. They need to be purposely put aside, otherwise they just hinder our desire to heal.

RUN YOUR RACE

The writer went on to encourage us to "run with endurance the race that is set before us" (v. 1). Many allow loss to define them for the rest of their lives. When we suffer loss, it's important to remember our race isn't finished yet. No quitting. What the writer was saying is that there's a race God has given each one of us to run; so run *your* race. We all have an astounding opportunity to present Christ to people, especially when He's entrusted us with trials. But you may say to yourself, "There is no way I can continue. How do I run this race?" The writer of Hebrews said there is a way.

FIXING OUR EYES ON JESUS

The only way to finish is by "fixing our eyes on Jesus" (v. 2). We must keep our eyes glued on the One who knows how to finish the race. It's Jesus himself who enables us to run, and keep on running, our race. He endured life on earth, suffered the humiliation of the cross, and finished with His eyes on the goal: salvation for all humankind. When you get weary and lose heart, and there will be those times, know there's help available. The Holy Spirit is our Helper who will see to it we make it through.

SALVATION OFFERED AND CLARIFIED

At this point it's important to ask, do you have a comforter? A guide to truth? A counselor without error? Are you trying to do any of this without help—supernatural help? Do you have *the* Helper? Whom are you trusting? What is its source?

If you're acquainted with the Savior, He's given this to you, and more: "But when the Friend comes, the Spirit of Truth, he will take you by the hand and guide you into all the truth there is. He won't draw attention to himself, but will make sense out of . . . all that I have done and said. He will honor me" (John 16:12–14 MSG).

Whenever a crisis or catastrophe hits, one of the first things people are told to do is assess their resources, their support systems. Can these hold up against the odds, the onslaught? The answer to this can determine the success of their recovery and their ability to rebuild their lives.

GOD'S PLAN AT WORK, PLAYING ITSELF OUT

In Matthew 10, Jesus had just finished giving His disciples their instructions for service—what to expect and how to conduct themselves. It was their first experience without training wheels (He wouldn't be present to oversee their practice), and He wanted to paint a realistic picture.

He was sending them off after spending time teaching them, demonstrating for them, and giving them guided practice, but now He needed to provide them with independent experience, on-the-job training. He gave them some authority, a few warnings about real life as a disciple—not romantic notions—and guidance on how to respond effectively for everyone's benefit.

In Matthew 11, Jesus was speaking to several audiences: John's disciples, the multitude, and the people with unrepentant hearts who lived in those cities where He performed miracles. Jesus' instruction to John's disciples about His calling was direct: "Go and report to John what you hear and see: the blind receive sight and the lame walk, the lepers are cleansed . . . the dead are raised up, and the poor have the gospel preached to them" (vv. 4–5). He made one more statement, "And blessed is he who does not take offense at Me" (v. 6). Jesus isn't always what we expect or want, but Jesus is always what we need.

As His own disciples were going away in His name, He turned His attention to the multitude and spoke about John the Baptist, asking them, "What did you go out into the wilderness to see? A reed shaken by the wind? . . . A man dressed in soft clothing . . . a prophet?" (vv. 7–9). He then reminded them how John's ministry was prophesied by God's Word in other times. John was sent to prepare the way for those who were willing to follow Jesus.

He then followed this by saying:

> To what shall I compare this generation? It is like children sitting in the market places, who call out to the other children, and say, "We played the flute for you, and you did not dance; we sang a dirge, and you did not mourn." For John came neither eating nor drinking, and they say, "He has a demon!" The Son of Man [Jesus] came eating and drinking, and they say, "Behold, a gluttonous man and a drunkard, a friend of tax collectors and sinners!" Yet wisdom is vindicated by her deeds. (vv. 16–19)

This last statement about wisdom refers to those things we judge too quickly but learn of their validity through real-life experience.

At this point, people had heard about John being in prison for doing what was right and fulfilling his call. Even John wasn't sure of the answer to whether Jesus was the One. So his question is universal for all who experience trials and unfair treatment: Is this really it, or should we look for someone else? Are *you* the Messiah, my Savior? What's the attraction, we may wonder.

Again, "blessed" is he or she who keeps from stumbling over *this* Savior. The prophets and men of God before John were mistreated, and the disciples after Jesus will be. Jesus himself was allowed by God to suffer and die at the hands of cruel men. Is this really the plan? The best the Creator of the universe has to offer? That sentiment echoes in our own times, "this generation."

In Matthew 11:20–24, Jesus reproached those cities "in which most of His miracles were done, because they did not repent." The resounding "Woe to you!" was applied to those without excuse. Even the wicked cities—Tyre, Sidon, and Sodom—will receive more mercy on the day of judgment because Jesus didn't do those works of God in their midst.

Finally, in Matthew 11:25–30, Jesus praised the Father for hiding His truth from the "wise and intelligent" and "revealing it to infants." Coming to faith in Jesus is an act that doesn't require great intellect or natural gifts. Believing in the Son of God requires ears that can hear and eyes that can see. In other words, being open to the Holy Spirit who makes this message from God clear and available to anyone who will receive it and "come." Jesus expects those to come who are weary, heavy-laden, and who want rest for their souls.

Are you tired of trying to do this job of living yourself? Then you're a perfect candidate. Jesus is inviting you: "Come to Me." The Father, Lord of heaven and earth, hides these truths from the proud and shows them to those without pretense. This is well-pleasing in God's sight: simple admission of need and simple faith given. Are you ready to believe God and receive the gift of His Son by faith?

These are familiar words of Jesus: "Take my yoke upon you and learn from Me, for I am gentle and humble in heart, and you will find rest for your souls" (v. 29). He knows all things—your circumstances, your disappointments and failures, and especially your heartbreak. In comparison to living life without a Redeemer and Friend, His "yoke is easy" and His "load is light."

If you've never surrendered to the One who made you and promises to provide what you really need, this is your opportunity. Ask Him to take charge of the overwhelming mess, the crushing load, the unending desires unfulfilled. It's been exhausting and impossible without Him. Let Him love you and relieve you of all burdens. It's what He came to do. His promised strength and everlasting grace is your only hope when life shows you its worst.

Let Him pick up the pieces, the shards and places of brokenness, and raise your eyes to see Him and His glory. He is sufficient for anything and waits to hold you now and always. Let Him have all of you, and walk in step with Him. Trust His character and words. There is light and life, refreshing and renewal. It's a promise.

APPENDIX A
by His design—A RECOVERY PLAN

After you've completed all parts of this material on dealing with loss, you're ready to take a private inventory. It's a tool to provide specific, personal accountability and show areas that still need growth. Honestly evaluate your progress in each case.

Everything covered should be familiar now, and the important thing to do is listen to the Spirit's voice and let the Lord put together a pattern of responses to walk in that may be somewhat new.

We've come a long way together, and it's the Father's job to make all this real for you. Ask Him to help you when you feel overwhelmed, and take breaks before coming back to finish. He'll still be there to complete His plan to wholeness.

STAY IN THE WORD

What are you going to study in God's Word?

When during the day?

Where?

How will you sustain this?

Where do you see other desperate people in the Bible?

What do they teach you?

PRAY HONESTLY AT ALL TIMES

What weighs you down?

What keeps you from praying honestly?

What do you know about God that encourages honest, regular prayer?

How can this become a habit?

FEEL THE PAIN

Are there areas where you are avoiding pain?

Why?

How will you address them?

What positive steps can you take to create healthy responses?

TAKE CARE OF YOURSELF

When can you exercise?

Where?

Are you eating healthy?

Is nutrition a part of your lifestyle?

How many hours of sleep do you get each night?

How are you having fun with friends who accept you "as is"?

READ OR TAKE A CLASS

What interests you?

Are there new skills you'd like to pursue?

What community resources can you take advantage of?

What books are on your reading list?

BE ARMED TO STAND

What attacks are you aware of?

Is there an area where you need to stand?

Who can support you in this?

Do you have questions about spiritual warfare (Eph. 6)?

FIND YOUR CALLING AND BUILD THE KINGDOM

What are your spiritual gifts?

What talents can you use for the kingdom?

Is there something you are uniquely prepared to do?

What is your heart telling you to do?

THROW OFF EVERYTHING THAT HINDERS YOUR RACE

What hinders you in your race?

How can you throw off those things?

Where are you seeing Jesus in the race?

CONSIDER HIM

Jesus endured opposition and did not grow weary and lose heart.

What are you convinced of?

What causes you to grow?

Do you believe He can defeat your enemy?

Are you feeling weary? If so, how can you find strength?

LOOK TO THE HORIZON AND DON'T FEAR

How has fear limited you?

How can you remind yourself that God is a loving God?

What Scripture verses help you remember God's love and His care for you?

Write these verses on an idex card and read them when you need reassurance.

ENTER AND POSSESS THE LAND

How has the Lord fought for you?

How did the Good Shepherd carry you?

What areas of your walk are not yoked to the Savior?

WHEN YOU'VE SAID, "I'M DONE; I CAN'T GO ON"

When you feel this way, how can you lean into Him?

Need a nap?

What other types of breaks can you take?

INTIMACY AND PERSEVERANCE GO HAND IN HAND

How are you fostering intimacy with God?

What steps can you take to know Him better?

ASK, "WHAT'S NOT WORKING, WHAT'S MISSING?"

What frustrations do you have?

What is their source?

What can you *not* change?

What can you change?

GARDEN ANALOGY

Weeds: How are you giving attention to these unwanted intruders?

What motivation do you have?

Compost pile: Are you processing "waste" into healthy matter each season?

What difficult areas want to harden into unmanageable issues?

On whom can you rely to help you?

WHAT ADDITIONAL HELPS CAN YOU IDENTIFY?

1.

2.

3.

4.

5.

CIRCLE THE CONCERN THAT NEEDS WORK

- Surrender.
- Develop head to heart communication.
- Expect purpose.
- Value supernatural realities.
- Worship.
- Be still.
- Rest.
- Praise.
- Hold all things loosely.
- Use your gifts and talents.
- Find role models.
- Let music minister with its message and beauty.
- Pray unceasingly, while letting God control and sustain.
- Exercise choices and accept God's way out in temptation.
- Know your limitations.
- Keep your eyes focused outward as you choose faith in difficult circumstances.
- Forgive.
- Remember that it's all about Him.
- Practice intimacy with the living God.
- Live deep, not shallow.
- Exercise the power and authority that exist in Jesus' name.
- Desire to make each day count.
- Hear His voice and wait on Him.
- Taste His goodness.

APPENDIX B
ABOUT *by His design*

The phrase *by His design* means God is sovereign which is the foundational truth in this book. That can be a difficult concept for people to accept—God is in control, always. God has a plan from beginning to end, and we fit into it. When the losses started accumulating in my life, because I (Beth) knew that somehow God was going to move me out to witness to His work of grace in this season, I began responding to the Spirit's promptings by writing to help others. Dave joined me in this new venture using his strengths, as we have the same heart for discipleship. God used our unique gifts and talents together. Consequently, our teaching is in the form of discipleship when loss, in its many forms, is introduced as a part of life.

Five areas of outreach have emerged so far: church settings, military and prison populations, overseas missions to the disadvantaged and underserved, disaster relief, and secular and Christian-based conferences. We all have broken hearts. It's how we deal with the brokenness that determines whether we dwell in life of loss.

We offer "grief relief" in a variety of ways and basically make what we do fit any need by teaching an assortment of workshops in different venues. For instance, we partner with Prison Fellowship in their Transformational Ministry Program, targeting those expected to be released immediately following graduation from this year-long commitment. The objective is to show them how to be transformed from the inside out, and therefore reduce the recidivism rate. In church settings, we speak to Sunday school classes, men's and women's gatherings, or in church services.

When we go overseas, we partner with missions groups, such as New Hope International in Eastern Europe. It was our privilege to minister to oppressed churches in Turkey, the Transnistria region, and Moldova. Military ministry, and the overwhelming need to aid families of soldiers who've been impacted by the conflicts in Iraq and Afghanistan, remains close to our hearts. God has used us at local retreats and national conferences in this regard. In addition, He is making a way by leading us to find suffering populations in disaster relief. We've completed specialized chaplain training and have deployed with Billy Graham's Rapid Responders and Samaritan's Purse. Recently we offered a variety of teaching in Haiti to locals in still-devastated Port-au-Prince, Samaritan's Purse staff and volunteers, along with training ministry leaders, using this workshop material.

In all this, what we've discovered from a biblical perspective captures the unspoken cry of those in turmoil—a lasting embrace that holds us close and lifts us up. Boundless mercy and compassion, power and strength are offered at just the right time. When life unravels, we need to assess the damage and create new avenues of support and stability. Questions surface: Is God there? Who else cares? What do I have control of? What does love look like? We have wrestled with and battled through such questions, and now we help others gain understanding, consider and incorporate practical strategies for survival, and develop a recovery plan to redeem a life filled with meaning and purpose.

Over our decades of life together, we have worked in full-time ministry, business, and public education for over thirty years. Now in "retirement," God is using our season of loss to provide hope and healing. *By His design* is a discipleship ministry to those seeking authentic answers to life's pressing questions, and our Lord connects us to the afflicted who are open to a biblical point of view and want help. Our websites—byhisdesignonline.com and besomeoneshero.org (our nonprofit and sending vehicle)—give detailed information and history of this outreach.

The efforts of *by His design* include a virtual presence as well. To take advantage of this opportunity, sign up for our weekly blog, monthly newsletter, or online curriculum, which offers facilitator training, as well as online cources related to our books. Enroll on the website or sign up at any of our workshops.

THE ONE-DAY WORKSHOP

A one-day workshop (or online course), *The Way of Hope: Growing Close to God through Loss*, from which this material is taken, is available for churches and other organizations who desire to help their hurting members. It provides a framework to see grace in action as God does His best work. Those who participate will benefit as they:

- Explore the implications of loss in life;
- Discover practical strategies for understanding how to walk through pain and confusion toward renewal and growth;
- Find out how to avoid pretending and connect with God's promises in authentic ways; and
- Learn to battle through grief with a recovery plan.

This event has been given in settings locally, nationally, and internationally. Please contact us through the website for information on how to book a workshop or other speaking events.

Other books from *by His design* include:

Hope in the Midst of Loss
I Am: An Unchanging God in a World of Change
What Do Daddies in Heaven Do? A Grief Resource List for Families

Discover the Way of Hope

Follow the way of hope with your group—in your church, home, or community—and travel together alongside Beth and Dave Weikel as they lead you through the dark paths of loss toward the true light, found only in God's Word. They themselves have passed the way of tragic loss several times and have found that, through the pain and brokenness, God's promises in Scripture become so much more meaningful.

DVD video teachings, combined with online facilitator resources and the follow-up devotional, *Hope in the Midst of Loss*, make for a transformational group discipleship journey while passing through the valley of the shadow of loss.

The Way of Hope
978-1-63257-050-5

The Way of Hope DVD
978-0-89827-886-6

Hope in the Midst of Loss
978-0-89827-998-6